A Checklist for the Children

Children will do what is expected of them. They often do their jobs more reliably than adults if they know the what, why, where, when, and how of them. Hang up the following list in some conspicuous spot.

- [ ] I help clean our house!
- [ ] I make my own bed.
- [ ] I hang up my own clothes and put them away.
- [ ] I put dirty clothes in the hamper.
- [ ] I pick up my toys when I'm done with them for the day.
- [ ] I scrape my plate after I eat and take it to the sink/dishwasher.
- [ ] I take my own things out of the car when we go somewhere.
- [ ] I put trash in the garbage right away, and I put empty cans and bottles in the recycle bin.
- [ ] I help fold clothes and do the laundry.
- [ ] I sweep/dust mop the floor.
- [ ] I help keep my pets clean.
- [ ] I dust.
- [ ] I help vacuum.

Cleaning Champion!

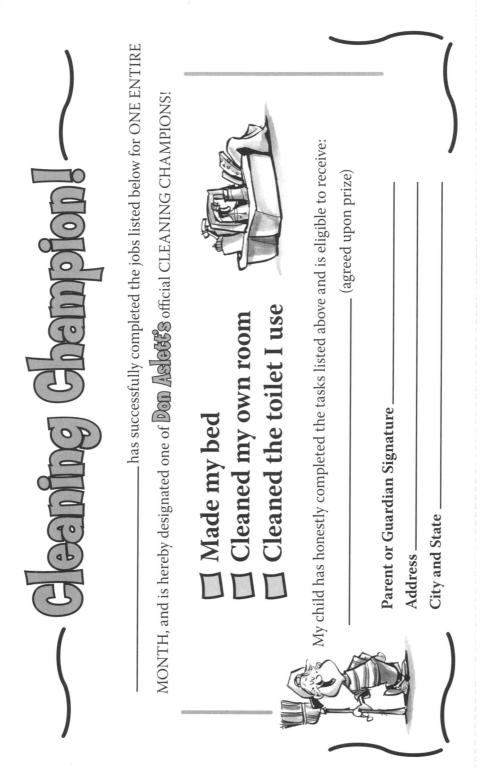

_____ has successfully completed the jobs listed below for ONE ENTIRE MONTH, and is hereby designated one of **Don Aslett's** official CLEANING CHAMPIONS!

- ☐ **Made my bed**
- ☐ **Cleaned my own room**
- ☐ **Cleaned the toilet I use**

My child has honestly completed the tasks listed above and is eligible to receive:

_____ (agreed upon prize)

_____
Parent or Guardian Signature

Address _____

City and State _____

OTHER DON ASLETT BOOKS
FROM ADAMS MEDIA

Clutter's Last Stand, 2nd Edition

Do I Dust or Vacuum First?, 2nd Edition

The Office Clutter Cure, 2nd Edition

Pet Clean-Up Made Easy, 2nd Edition

*DONE! How to Accomplish Twice as Much in
Half the Time—at Home and at the Office!*

Weekend Makeover

Is There Life After Housework?, 2nd Edition

Published by Adams Media, an F+W Publications Company
57 Littlefield Street
Avon, MA 02322
www.adamsmedia.com

Printed in Canada.
ISBN: 1-59337-508-5

Library of Congress Cataloging-in-Publication Data
Aslett, Don
Help! around the house : a mother's guide to getting the family
to pitch in and clean up / Don Aslett.
p. cm.
ISBN 1-59337-508-5
1. House cleaning. 2. Communication in the family. 3. Family. I. Title.
TX324.A75824 2006
648'.5--dc22
2005026448

This publication is designed to provide accurate and authoritative information with
regard to the subject matter covered. It is sold with the understanding that the publisher
is not engaged in rendering legal, accounting, or other professional advice. If legal advice
or other expert assistance is required, the services of a competent professional person
should be sought.

—From a *Declaration of Principles* jointly adopted by a
Committee of the American Bar Association and
a Committee of Publishers and Associations

Many of the designations used by manufacturers and sellers to distinguish their products are claimed as trademarks. Where those designations appear in this book and Adams
Media was aware of a trademark claim, the designations have been printed with initial
capital letters.

Cover illustration by Tad Herr.
Interior illustrations by jimhunt.us.

*This book is available at quantity discounts for bulk purchases.
For information, please call 1-800-872-5627.*

HELP!
Around the House

A Mother's Guide to Getting
the Family to Pitch in and Clean Up

Don Aslett
America's #1 Cleaning Expert

Adams Media
Avon, Massachusetts

Contents

Introduction

It was an hour before the beginning of one of my popular *"Is There Life After Housework?"* stage shows. I was setting up my props and adjusting the mike when one early-arriving attendee eased up to me to explain why she was attending this cleaning show and seminar. "My husband went to a lot of trouble to buy me a ticket for this, and made sure I came . . . while he and the kids are home causing the mess that I came here to learn how to handle better."

She was in the right place but for the wrong reason. Her husband definitely didn't buy enough tickets; he was (as many men and children were, or still are) under the impression that it's a woman's job to clean.

I wasn't at all surprised by her comment. There has long been a need for a solution to "the cleaning problem"—the fact that home cleaning is done by women, no matter who else lives in the home. When it comes to cleaning, we don't need charts, studies, and certificates of proof. We see the truth and live it every day of the week. The evidence is before our eyes, everywhere. Men and children create most housework, and women do most of the cleaning. That's it—pure and simple. Even when they work outside the home, women still do most of the cooking, cleaning, child care, and errands.

> "A clean home benefits the whole family, so we stress that cleaning and chores are something on which the whole family pitches in. Keeping our house clean so that it feels like a home is not just something Mom does. After all, Mom isn't usually the one making most of the dirt or mess! I remind my children that they are needed—there is no way I can keep up our home all by myself."

I began my own involvement in cleaning, the world's oldest and largest profession, fifty years ago as a professional cleaner, and now I am "America's #1 Cleaning Expert." When I enrolled in college at nineteen, I put an ad in the paper to help me work my way through. The ad read, "Need housecleaning or yard work done? Call Don Aslett, 239-1269." Soon I was cleaning houses and anything else people wanted, for $1.25 an hour. When I got more work than I could handle, I hired one of my fellow students to help, then two, ten, twenty, and more. We would invade a home and wash all the walls, strip and wax floors, shampoo the rugs and upholstery, clean the windows, and often do painting inside and out. Soon we were also doing fire and flood restoration, cleaning vandalized homes, and even tackling the chaos of kids' rooms! This little cleaning company, called Varsity Contractors, grew as I worked my way toward my degree. By the time I graduated, I knew more about cleaning than I did about philosophy or dissecting frogs, so I stayed in the business of cleaning. Today, my company does cleaning and maintenance in all fifty states and Canada, with thousands of employees and subcontractors (smaller cleaning firms) under its umbrella.

I might be weird, but I love cleaning, and to share my passion I started writing articles and speaking about cleaning to groups and clubs. Encouraged by the enthusiastic response of my audiences (at least 90 percent of whom at first were women), I wrote and self-published a book called, *Is There Life After Housework?* A national publisher, Writer's Digest Books, soon republished it and it became a best seller. (For thirty giddy days it was even ahead of *The Joy of Sex* and *30 Days to a Beautiful Bottom* on the bestseller list.) In those days (the early 1980s), good books soon put you in the media spotlight, and I appeared on thousands of radio and television shows and in hundreds of newspaper stories. People loved the novelty of a man telling the women of the world how they could clean faster, better, and even more cheaply.

I gave "Life After Housework" seminars all over the country and in the process collected over 180,000 comment cards from home cleaners. The cards asked things like the size of home, size of family, and who did the housework. The answers, comments, and requests on these, coming directly from the home front as they did, were rich, rich ore that I used to write my second book, 100 questions and answers about housework, titled *Do I Dust or Vacuum First?* It too soon became a bestseller.

At this point, it was clear from my media appearances and letters from readers that one of the toughest, most time-consuming tasks around was dealing with household junk and clutter. So I wrote a book to help people combat the stuff buildup, called *Clutter's Last Stand*, the first book ever on this very modern subject and one that has sold more than three quarters of a million copies.

Next I did a groundbreaking book addressed to men, *Who Says It's a Woman's Job to Clean?*, designed to encourage husbands to assume some of the household load. And now, more than two dozen books later, I'm finally addressing perhaps the most frustrating problem of all in home cleaning—getting kids (as well as husbands and mates) to assume some of the responsibility for the cleaning and upkeep of the home.

Am I qualified to speak out on this great unsolved mystery? This often discouraging but important subject? Who better?

I am the leading guru of cleaning in this country. Not only have I been a professional cleaner for half a century and an outspoken champion of the often unappreciated role of the home cleaner, but my wife and I also raised a big family of our own. We had six children, as well as foster children and young guests from other countries often staying with us (we had eight teenagers living in the house at once at one point). We often had more than a dozen young people at a time sleeping over or camping out at our house, and youth parties with more than a hundred attending. Now I have eighteen grandchildren that sometimes storm the house at once. I've lived and researched this subject intensely because I knew it was one that would help families everywhere.

Throughout the course of my cleaning career I've had the opportunity to tour dormitories full of all kinds of young people, from those in Olympic villages to large universities. I've traveled and lived with Scouts across the country (nothing is grubbier than a Scout tent). I've cleaned mansions, bunkhouses, and plain old ordinary houses—seven-bedroom houses and tiny mobile homes that were home to seven kids. I've cleaned up after every imaginable type and status of person, including the Kennedy kids from Boston. As my interest in inspiring kids to clean their rooms grew, I began teaching grade school, junior high, and high school assemblies on the subject, from Alaska to Cincinnati.

More than twenty-five years ago, I began putting together a book tentatively titled "How to Get Kids to Clean Their Rooms." Yet nowhere on my list of published books (more than thirty) could you find a book on this subject—until now. Why? I think you know the answer already. I couldn't find a solution, one that really worked.

For decades I gathered opinions, anecdotes, options, stories, and studies on this subject. I had baskets and boxes of videos, books, and comment cards. I had files full of magazine articles and interviews with child psychologists. My "Kids Cleaning" research file was enormous. There was some good stuff here and there, but it was buried in a ton of words, theories, philosophies, and idealistic shoulds and shouldn'ts. Despite all of these tips and tricks, kids were cleaning less than ever.

The more I delved into kid cleaning, the more I found that everyone struggles with it, even the wonder women and model dads. To make matters worse, there are new boundaries and premises now. In the old days, it was easier to find help and distribute work around the house because chores for children were taken for granted. There are some big hurdles to get over now in coming up with a good answer.

- "Clean" is a hard sell; it always has been. The lack of glory in housework and the impermanence of the results are just two of the strikes against it.
- The combination of availability, convenience, and lenient credit today has resulted in almost all of us owning too much stuff, which we then have to sort through, care for, and store.
- We have more room today. Larger houses, closets, garages, and yards mean more opportunity for mess and more places to clean.
- Everyone is more distracted than ever with multitudes of other options—hundreds, if not thousands, of things to do, watch, and play with—so why waste time cleaning? We are all (even the little ones) busy today if not buried.
- Men or kids of any age are not very likely to sit down and read and then follow a book about modifying messy behavior and doing chores.
- Our modern culture is almost devoid of authority. No one wants to take a chance of offending anyone, or taking a firm stand on anything.

I seem to be building a pyramid of impossibility here, creating the impression that perhaps this business of getting everyone in the family to help can never be solved. Is it an impossible dream? Not at all—I'm only reminding us of why good answers have eluded us.

One of the most useful and smartest things I did in my research was to ask for the input and opinions of my longtime readers, as well as the people who buy cleaning supplies from my mail-order company. I was overwhelmed, not only by the number of responses, but also by the quality of the wisdom they contained. I wasn't just heartened—I was awed. I was raised in a large family, had worked with kids all my life, and figured I knew a lot after fifty years of this. After reading all of those letters and e-mails, I felt like a beginner. The material we received was so good, we delayed the book another month to process and include as much of it as we could.

At last, I could complete this thirty-years-overdue book about getting kids to clean!

I am an opinionated person, as any of you who have read my other books know. I've made my own views clear in these pages, but I've included some alternate views as well. When our own strategies fail to deliver, perhaps it's time to try someone else's. Some of my readers' solutions I've included aren't my style and won't be yours, but they may spark possibility and initiative and give you the courage to go for it and come up with something far better than mine *or* theirs.

You'll enjoy these ideas and find some beneficial, I'm sure. The most inspiring thing about them is that they are all from parents who know that everyone helping the household is important and are making an effort to accomplish it.

You probably wouldn't believe anyone, including me, who claimed to have all the answers for getting the rest of the family to help around the house. You may not find all of the answers here, but you will find insights and principles that will inspire and direct you to the results you want and need. You will find in these pages some different and (I hope) fresh ideas, some new leverage to take advantage of, and some new tools and approaches. Don't underestimate even the most off-the-wall ideas in here!

"We've made cleaning part of the responsibility of being a member of the family. If you live in the house, you help take care of it. It belongs to all of us."

Chapter 1

There Is Hope, So Take Heart!

We human beings are amazing creations—no two of us are exactly alike. But we all react about the same when we first face something that appears impossible. Our first thought is, "There's no way, man!" We only see it as something that can't be done, whether it's putting together a 2,500-piece jigsaw puzzle of a herd of zebras, climbing a 30,000-foot mountain, memorizing a 380-page script, feeding seventy-two people on an hour's notice, or painting a four-story house all by yourself in a weekend. Just as you've decided for sure not to attempt any of these, someone far less qualified tells and shows, not only how all of these things can be done, but how they can be done fast and well.

That is why I'm going to show right at the start that getting the rest of the family to help with home care not only can but *has* been done. No one may have their family 100-percent converted to helping clean, but there are 60, 75, and 90 percenters all over the place out there. If they can do it, you and I or any of us can do it. So listen up—there is not only hope, there are cleaner and less stress-filled homes all over. We will get to the hows later; right now, let's concentrate on the "it happeneds."

The first good glimpse I personally got of this was in the military. I saw it in ROTC in college, during my time in National Guard barracks and camps, and in the many people I've known in my life both before and after their time in military service. Completely unkempt, irresponsible, filthy-room Freds and Franks, slobs from toddlerhood, would enter any branch of the military. Within days, sometimes hours, their behavior changed. By the second night in Uncle Sam's service, their footlockers were neat, clothes clean, and their beds would bounce a quarter. They smelled clean, now, too, and were even saying "Sir" to their mothers (the original drill sergeants!). They changed lifetime habits and conduct in an area very unfamiliar to them. Of the more than half a million people I've had working for me over the past fifty years, I could usually pick out those who had been in the military. Their cleaning and painting gear was always clean and in order, and they put it away right after use. Or, as one ex-navy man put it, things were always "squared away."

Likewise, I've not only taught in schools (grade school, high school, and college) but I've also cleaned them, studied them, consulted on them, and served on school boards. And I've seen some interesting contrasts there, too.

Once, when I was doing a consulting study for a large Eastern school district, I was introduced to a quiet, clean, and shiny grade-school cafeteria. At the stroke of noon, 400 children converged enthusiastically on the room with trays and brown bags. Forty minutes later, the room was quiet again, but not polished. It looked like a tornado had feasted there instead of young humans. Forks, food, and wrappers decorated the floor, tables, chairs, walls, and even the light fixtures. When I was finishing up the building tour two hours later, I noticed the janitor just finishing the cleaning. Two thirty-gallon garbage cans were required to contain the mess the janitor picked up from that lunchroom.

The next day I was touring a similar school in the same town: same floor plan, and about the same number of students. This time I arrived fifteen minutes after lunch ended, and the cafeteria was immaculate! The janitor was scooping up what appeared to be the final dustpan of debris, and not only was it the final dustpan, it was the *only* dustpan! I mentioned that the other school had two janitors and it took them two hours and there were two bales of residue after every lunch.

He smiled proudly and said,

"It's simple, Mr. Aslett—it's the principal. South Side's principal has the attitude that they are educators and students and it's not the janitor's job to clean up after them all. My principal assembles the kids and teachers the first day and lays out the standards and expectations and carefully explains how everything is going to be. 'Anything you mess up, you clean up,' is his fair and simple rule. That means crumbs, wrappers, cans, and cartons, and drops and dribbles on tables, chairs, and floors. It takes each kid only seconds to do this!"

It worked. I saw it—his school was neat as a pin, while the other school was trashed by both the students and the teachers.

Which of these schools do you want your kids coming out of to face life—the one where his or her mess is always taken care of by someone else, or the one where kids are taught they are responsible for their own messes? Many times, school classrooms show this same difference. One is a pigsty, while the one right next door is clean and orderly. Both are used by the same age and grade of students, and often even the very same students. This should give us a clue in this cleaning quandary that maybe it isn't just the kids after all.

My company cleaned a high school in Arizona—a nice new high-end building in an upscale community. At 11:30 A.M. the hallway looked like a tunnel of glass, thanks to some of the best automatic floor polishers and highest-quality floor finishes the night before. By 12:30, lunchtime, you could barely see the floor. It was so covered with trash that it ran over the top of the dust mop when sweeping. Kids thought nothing of running markers down the wall, or emptying their lockers right there in the hall and just tossing stuff on the floor, not bothering to carry it to the wastebasket just ten feet away. In the cafeteria, if someone left an empty can or wrapper or some uneaten food on a table and someone else wanted to sit there, he would just rake it off onto the floor with his arm and then sit down to eat.

There is no question that sloppy behavior at home is brought out into the world and compounded, until someone, be it the military system or a good principal, refuses to tolerate it. Then bingo! The place is clean. It's all a matter of some simple expectations and leadership.

Another of my school experiences exceeded even my own often overly optimistic imaginings. I received a call from the superintendent of an Alaskan school district, who asked me to come up there and "shape up" the janitorial staff. (The school seemed to be deteriorating, and as usual, everyone blamed everything on the poor janitors.) I had the time and the fee was agreeable, so I told him I would do it on one condition. Before working with the janitors I wanted to first meet briefly with the administration and school board and then do some assemblies. There was a long silence on the line and then he said, "Assembly? What kind of assembly?" "A cleaning assembly," I replied. Another long silence and finally (like the response to most cleaning initiatives), he gave me a reluctant "Okay."

I knew that it was probably not so much the "mess fixers" (the janitors) as the mess makers who needed reeducating, so I decided to teach the children first . . . and it worked.

When I arrived in the wonderful state of Alaska, I did meet with the administration, the board, and some of the parents, and these meetings almost eliminated the need to meet with the janitors (another story). Then came the assembly. The cutest kids in the world assembled excitedly—tiny kinder-garteners at the front of the hall in rows on the floor, and big sixth graders in the back, and all of the teachers standing by the door with folded arms and irritated looks on their faces (probably because good school time was being taken up by something as silly as a cleaning assembly). I'd set the scene ahead of time by putting some hand smudges on the wall and leaving wads of paper and wrappers around.

Then I zipped onto the stage and introduced myself, "Hi, I'm Don Aslett, from Idaho. If anyone knows what Idaho is famous for, I'll give you a prize." Taken a little aback by this loud opener, they just blinked, until one kid finally said. "Potatoes!" "Right!" I yelled, running up to him and handing him a little souvenir Idaho potato pin. The kids were paying close attention now. (A prize always gets them.) Back on stage, I shouted, "Now if anyone here knows what I do for a living, I have another prize." Again quiet, and then one little charmer whose father or mother was probably in my earlier meeting shouted back, "You clean toilets!" The whole place burst into laughter, and I said, "You are right, young man, and you win a genuine miniature toilet keychain" (an exact replica, in plastic). Now I had them—they all wanted one!

I then gave a quick account of when I was a kid in school, how I learned to be neat and clean, and how that paid off. I told them I wrote books on cleaning and gave some books to the teachers to take back to class. This pleased the teachers and built some anticipation in the kids. Then I showed them how much fun cleaning could be by demonstrating how they could clean windows with a squeegee on an extension pole. Finally I asked if they could see anything wrong in the room.

A couple of kids spotted the hand smudges and I called one of them up, handed him a spray bottle and cloth, and asked him to clean up quick. The place went crazy and tried to spot other areas needing cleaning to win a tiny toilet or some of my other cleaning prizes (I also had toilet pencil sharpeners and toilet erasers). The teachers' arms were unfolded now and they were beaming with endorsement.

Now I called up two boys and messed one up—pulled his shirttail out, mussed his hair, turned his pockets wrong side out, undid his shoelaces, put a few smudges on his face, and put a little skunk stuffed animal under his arm and some rubber dog poop in his hand (much to the delight of the kids). I combed the other boy's hair perfect, neatened him up, decorated him a little, and then presented both of them to the group.

"If the president visited tomorrow, which of these boys would you want to greet him? Which would you want for a friend?" They all picked the neat kid, and that taught them another lesson.

Next I called up a little girl, handed her an open pint of chocolate milk, and bumped her arm, spilling the milk on a piece of carpet I had laid down. A fearful groan came from the audience. "Uh-oh," I yelled, "who do we call?" A chorus of voices came back, "Ghostbusters!" (Except for one little boy who said "the cat!") I held back my laugh and said, "No, they didn't do it, who do we call?" Some yelled back, "Mother!" "Nope, she didn't do it either." They were silent now. They didn't have an answer for that. "The person who spills something should clean it up," I said. This was the perfect moment to teach them how and why to clean up a spill quickly, safely, and effectively. The girl ended up by doing a tap dance on the cloth I'd put down to soak up the spill.

(I know this made an impression because two weeks later I got a call from the superintendent thanking me. He did mention that when one six-year-old got home from school, she ran to the fridge, got a quart of milk, and poured it out on the living room rug to show her mother what they learned in school today.)

With other little tricks and scenarios, I reinforced the message, "Kids can clean." I taught the kids lots of other things too, such as the uncouthness of chewing gum and clipping fingernails just anywhere, all leading up to the close, where I challenged one of the top athletes in the school to a toilet cleaning race. As I declared him the winner (I always make sure the child wins) I held the toilet seat up to frame his face. (This made for a picture that often got a full page in local papers all over the country.)

By now time was up and they got the message. Then it struck me that I might carry this a little further. So I held up one of the little toilets, "How many of you would like to have one of these?" Of course 100% percent of the hands reached high. "Okay, here's the deal." I waved a blank sheet of paper in the air and said, "I have here a certificate that asks you to do three things—Number one: Clean your own room. Do you think you can do that?" A big chorus of "Yes" came back. "Number two is make your bed. How many of you can do that?" An even bigger chorus of "Yes" came back. "Number three is clean the toilet you use. How many of . . ." "Yessss!"

"Okay, get a certificate from your teacher and take it home. If you do all three of these things perfectly every day for a month, without a miss, and bring it back signed by your parent or guardian, I'll send you a little toilet." Quickly after the assembly I typed up this little certificate. Then the teachers and I ran off a thousand of them on the copier.

I expected the enthusiasm to die away after I left town and thought I might eventually get a dozen or so responses (as we do when we ask adults to do such things). One month and four days later, (the time it took mail to get from Alaska

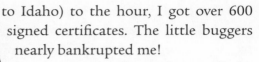

to Idaho) to the hour, I got over 600 signed certificates. The little buggers nearly bankrupted me!

In his thank-you phone call, the superintendent said that without question the cleaning assembly was the single best public relations move the school district had ever made.

So as this long story demonstrates, conversion to cleaning can work. I have since done cleaning assemblies all over the country, with the same results.

Here's one more short story now to reinforce my point. I am a big Scouting devotee and have served as the leader of forty Boy Scouts for three national Jamborees. Once, on the way to a jamboree campsite I had thirty boys staying in motels and hotels. I don't need to tell you how kids treat places like this—the beds, for example, become impromptu trampolines. The first morning, getting the kids up and into the bus without forgetting half the things their mothers made sure they had, I visited their rooms. It was a ghastly sight—there were socks hanging off light fixtures, towels all over the place, blankets and pillows on the floor, things tipped over, pizza crusts and popcorn all over, and nothing in the wastebasket. "Okay, this does not go for Scouts! One of the Scout laws is that a Scout is clean, so clean this place up. There will be no breakfast, no bus, no anything until this room is spiffy." (There was definitely a downside to traveling with "Mr. Clean," as they all nicknamed me.)

The response? "Hey, we *paid* for this room—they have to clean it!" "Right, boys, you pay to use it, not abuse it, so clean it up. I'll be back later." Luckily I was still new and scary to them, and their leader, so they did what I said, not only that morning, but the next one, too. Finally, they got the idea. On the fourth morning while we were checking out they told the manager and the people behind the desk, "Hey, go look at rooms 231 and 232. They are as clean as when we came in." The Scouts not only could and did clean, but they were proud of their accomplishment and wanted it acknowledged. It was a memorable moment for them and an assuring moment for me: There is hope, and people can change. They can learn to do home care and cleaning well and feel good about it. Here are some more examples from my readers if you're not convinced yet.

> "All six of our children have become very good at all types of cleaning jobs: windows, bathrooms, carpets, wooden floors, kitchens, dusting, you name it. Working alongside your children is such a pleasure. We do just about everything together."

> "My seventeen-year-old cleans his room, knows how to vacuum and mop, mows and trims the lawn, puts out the trash, and does his own laundry. My twenty-year-old is in college, and he often has to show clueless students how to wash their own clothes or iron a shirt."

> **"I am a single mother of four, and my kids do all the dishes, laundry, pet care, and trash, as well as most of the cleaning. They are very self-reliant and the major blessings in my life."**

> "Since there are thirteen children in our house, cleaning has always been a major time-consumer. Early on we knew that the children would need to play a large part in the process. Having started at a young age, the children accepted cleaning as a way of life, no different than putting on their own clothes in the morning."

There *is* a solution to the problem that has long plagued us. It begins by applying just two basic principles—expectation and involvement. Once these are enacted, the simple steps outlined in the following chapters—decluttering, designing housework out, deciding, describing, and then demonstrating—will all come together. Then the old attempts to deal with the problem by nagging and threatening can cease forever.

"Why I Think Kids Should Help," by the third graders
of Bright Elementary in Sugar Tree Ridge, Ohio

"If the kids made it messy they should pick it up!"

"It might be fun to clean the house."

"Because parents need help around the house."

"If the grownups have to do it all
by themselves it will take longer."

"Moms won't have to do so much work.
Moms get tired and we love our moms
so we should help."

"Because it's NICE to help."

"Because the house will be clean."

"Because it's your house too!"

"Because it's hard to clean by yourself."

"It would make me feel bad if no one helped *me*!"

Chapter 2
Why It **Must** Work

Let's go back to school again for a minute now. I was once speaking to a group of school principals and asked them to tell me what they considered the single most important, life-affecting principle or subject that a student leaving school must know. No one came up with an answer immediately, but you could see the wheels in the educators' brains turning. I pushed them a little—is it reading? Writing? Or arithmetic? Career or computer savvy? Something from health class? What is it? No one could come up with or agree on a clear-cut answer so I suggested one, and they all immediately agreed.

Regardless of age, intelligence, or cultural background, if a student leaves school knowing just one thing it will almost guarantee success. What is it? "I am responsible for my own actions." Once you accept ownership of your own actions and their consequences, you can work the rest of life out pretty well.

But if you come out of school and go out into life believing that there is always going to be someone out there to take care of things for you, to follow behind you and clean up your mess (your parents, nannies, the government, the church, the boss, the bank, the lawyers, and so on) it's bad news. Young people go off to college to learn how to manage a business when they can't even manage the aftermath of their own daily grooming. When they find themselves fouled up—scholastically, financially, socially, or emotionally—they don't know what to do, because someone has always looked after their needs before. Forever picking up after kids or anyone else is the most character-weakening thing you can do, for it teaches them that they don't have to answer for their own behavior.

> No college class at Harvard or Yale can teach our
> children management and discipline if we have
> allowed them a lifetime of doing nothing.

The biggest reason women shouldn't have to do all the cleaning is the unspoken assumption that cleaning is in fact their job. Being cleaned up after is in effect saying LET SOMEBODY ELSE DO IT!

Every pattern and attitude we acquire in one area of our life carries over into other areas. If we dodge our chores as kids, we're likely to do the same in our marriage and our career. If we grow up wasting things, we may well be wasteful of time and life later. The quitter on the kids' leaf-raking team will probably be the quitter on the sales-analysis team at work. People who never learned to see a mess around them won't recognize a problem when it happens in their business, health, or marriage.

We spend most of our time at home. If we learn there to ignore commitments and promises, to be insensitive to others' needs, we'll carry those habits right along with us to the outside world.

Each one of my Boy Scout Jamboree trips that I mentioned earlier was like escorting forty little tornadoes. Every place we stopped—every eating area, every motel room we left—was a spoil of litter and trash. Ten Scouts take a break and what do you find? Eleven pop cans! They can expand a single six-pack of soda or package of snacks into forty square feet of rubbish. On the ground, under and around every outdoor table we ate at were mashed ketchup packets, half-eaten food, wrappers, napkins, plastic forks and spoons, straws, and twisted, wrinkled magazines and books. The tents often looked like someone threw the contents of a Salvation Army store into a blender and dumped the mess a foot deep on the floor. Every empty film container, crumpled tissue, and inkless pen was dropped, left, or laid right where someone finished with it. I asked one bright-eyed fourteen-year-old, "Doesn't this mess bother you?" His answer: "What mess?"

And remember we're talking about Scouts here—healthy, honorable, good family youth.

Once, as I was sitting at a table in a large Scout camp dining hall, the head of the camp came in. He plugged his electric razor into the socket between the tables, shaved with it, then took the razor head off and blew whiskers all over the tables and clean floor.

If we only did housework for one reason—the incalculable value of carryover—it would be worth it.

Cleaning: A Key to Personal Success

Learning to clean after yourself is a prime key to personal success. If we allow and accept slobby standards in our children, at home or wherever else they may go, we'll have guaranteed carryover into the way they write, speak, drive, play, work, and handle money, as well as their relationships with others. Somewhere down the line, how they clean will be how they live. Does that make it seem important enough—enough of a priority that they learn to clean?

Kids' cleaning is not an option or nicety. It's a necessity. If children don't learn, it'll plague them the rest of their lives. My friend Gladys Allen once said about talented kids, "What good is a concert violinist if he can't fold towels?" Our first response might be that we'd take such an exceptional talent over cleaning skills, but the inability to look after oneself affects every area of a person's life, eventually. Knowing how to take care of yourself in your everyday environment is a skill no one should be without—it's even more important than knowing how to entertain yourself!

We often excuse kids from cleaning for reasons like, "Mom, if I don't do this homework, I won't pass the exam!" But that is actually short-range logic. If a young man doesn't do his housework, he won't pass life's requirements. What in the long run is going to affect a person more, a grade on a test or the sense of responsibility gained from learning to handle the consequences of his actions? No one is too busy, too rich, or too important to close the drawer she just opened, to hang up clothes she just wore, to make the bed she just slept in, to clean up a dish she just ate from, put her own trash in a container, or close the door she just passed through.

Think for a minute how pathetic it is for anyone else, even a janitor, to have to come in and clean up a mess you have created. While doing the Alaskan school assembly I called the janitor up in front of the room and asked the audience, "Who is this?" "Mr. Wicket, the janitor!" the kids chorused back. "What is his job?" "He cleans the school!" "No," I yelled back, "that is not his job. His job is to maintain the building. He didn't dirty it up, why should he clean it?" That stumped the kids—they had never heard such a heresy. "It is *your* job to clean it. Mr. Wicket dumps the wastebaskets, but it isn't his job to pick trash up from all over. He mops and waxes the floors and fixes the broken doorknobs and keeps things running. He vacuums the mats, but it is your job to wipe your feet on them."

The same is true of a mother at home. She has scores of other things to deal with, from the family's health and finances to social concerns. She shouldn't have to clean up behind other family members.

I think the "Adopt a Highway" program is one of the worst ideas ever. The program supports mess-makers. Instead of "Adopt a Highway," the sign should read "Adopt a Habit (of Taking Care of Your Own Mess)." Continually cleaning up after people is like taking a detention or getting a vaccination for them. The other person learns nothing, gets no benefit, and only has it worse in the end when he finally has to face his bad habits.

Cleaning Creates a Pattern of Consideration

Cleaning is more than just the physical arrangement of objects; it involves the mental arrangement of our lives, and habits that make us happy or sad. When you think about it, you'll find that the concepts of order and neatness have profound power. You aren't teaching an act; you are teaching a principle of self-responsibility. The actual picking up is just the mechanics of it. The spirit of it is consideration, kindness, self-respect, and service. That is what cleaning is all about. Cleaning can set a pattern for the organization and responsibility in our children's whole lives. If we fail to do this now, we may never have the chance again.

We aren't doing kids a favor by letting them think that a home is kept clean by magic or perhaps by unseen elves.

This is what happens when you do all the work after the kids go to bed—when they get up, the house is ready for them to undo again. They will grow up to be users of society and other people. And to think that *you*, well educated and caring as you are, carefully taught them that day after day after day. Kids don't absorb responsibility from lectures and peers; they have to be taught it. Cleaning is the best tool around—it beats television and textbooks by far.

> "A little mess doesn't hurt them; after all, it's their room. They have to live with it. They'll grow out of it when a mate, the military, or the dorm master gets their hands on them. I guess by the same token a little malnourishment won't hurt them either. After all, it is their body, and they'll have to live with it. They'll grow out of all of those chemical- and sugar-saturated foods and drinks, and they can always get transplants, false teeth, surgery, or a wheelchair."

Is It Mean to Ask Kids to Clean?

Let me dispel any hint of abuse or cruelty on our part in requiring kids to clean. Cleaning isn't hard, and it isn't an option in life. It's a necessity. Teaching children discipline isn't an act of revenge or way of torturing them—it is their only salvation in the 10,000-path world of this new century. Those who cannot or will not take responsibility for themselves and control their own habits will not be happy, productive adults. I've known hundreds of people who had to work, or "do chores," at home when they were children, and some even went through some tough times of not getting everything they wanted or thought they needed. All of them—100 percent—now look back with pleasure and thankfulness for what those early days did for them.

Whether children help clean, not only has a big impact on how much cleaning

will need to be done in a home over the years, but also on what our young people will be like later in life.

The Last Frontier of Home Learning

In earlier years, many of us lived in rural settings, and everyone in the family had to lend a hand to help the family survive. Children, too, had many jobs and assignments.

When I was a boy we all had chores—important, precious chores to do. There was coal to fetch, water to carry, animals to herd and feed, cows to milk, potatoes to pick, and beans to weed (fields and fields of them, which we attacked enthusiastically as a family). It was a real adventure to tromp the hay in the loft or the grain in the bins. I saw hard work at ten, and by the age of twelve I graduated to a full man's workload.

Gone are the days of doing the chores—gathering eggs or firewood, working in the fields or garden, and hanging out the clothes. (Most kids today don't even know what a clothesline is.) Now few kids even get to see a farm, so cleaning up after themselves and others is one of the few "schools of life" left.

Cleaning is one of the last opportunities children have around the home to learn personal responsibility and to help the family cope with the daily demands of living. These days most things are done for us—we have automatic sprinklers, garden tillers, leaf blowers, snow blowers, dishwashers, automatic washers and dryers, power saws, and power screwdrivers, and remote controls to turn the channel. We hardly have to turn a hand to get along just fine. Automation has eliminated hundreds of jobs we once had to share with our children, along with the skills and principles that went with them. The several-mile walk to school in the old days is now a luxury ride in the family car or school bus, insulated from the weather. Things open by themselves, cook by themselves, and mind themselves. So where can a child find the satisfaction of doing something that needs to be done and feeling good about it afterward? Teaching kids to clean at home is a chance to instill a work ethic—no one else is doing it!

The home is the first and finest classroom.

What Are Our Goals?

Before we launch into the details of getting kids to clean, let's take a minute to put our goals in perspective:

1. **A home is to live in, not live for.** We sometimes pay more attention to what the house looks like than who lives in it. Kids use and appreciate a home more than most adults. As we grow older, our home often becomes more a matter of vanity, necessity, and financial burden. But kids love homes, so let them use their houses to grow and do! If we had more fingerprints on the walls at home, we'd have less on the police blotters downtown.

2. **There is nothing wrong with making a mess.** If kids are going to learn to build and overhaul, sew, paint, invent, whittle, or wrestle—do just about anything—they are going to create some kind of mess. Mess is creativity's constant shadow. Cooking, having pets, and pursuing projects all mean messes. Making a mess is no crime. It's part of life, and often the bigger the mess, the bigger the blessing. The problem is not in making a mess but in leaving it behind for someone else.

3. **The real goal in all of this is better kids and family,** not cleaner closets.

"External discipline becomes self-discipline later in life."

Remember the Multiplication Factor

The bad news is that it might not be easy to get the rest of the household swung over to sweeping up after themselves or other housework. However, when you do get even just get one little habit ingrained, it is never for just one time. Take sock turning, for example. If you can get everyone to turn their socks right side out before dropping them in the hamper, extended out to the rest of a child's or husband's life, that means 10,000 times you don't have to do it,—a nice yield for a single effort up front. Once the old "Scrape your dish and take it to the sink" habit is in place, it isn't just in place for that meal, on that day—instead, it is good for 1,000 meals a year, and forty, fifty, or 60,000 in a lifetime.

"I raised boys and for some reason thought boys shouldn't have to clean up their rooms, make their beds, etc., because they had so many more important things to do. Just close the doors to their rooms and love them unconditionally. Ha! One boy did turn into a neat freak, probably in self-defense, but the other one to this day is untidy, his wife is untidy, and visiting their house is painful. I should have started with little steps when they were very young, so neatness would have been ingrained. Sign me anonymous."

"I assume that patience works—all I know is what DOESN'T work. Since I was too impatient to train him and did all the work for him, I now have a spoiled, lazy twenty-five-year-old on my hands."

"I wish my parents had trained me younger. I've learned a lot of these skills only later in life (thanks to your books, Don!)."

"My dear mother did all my tidying and cleaning for me; I now wish she hadn't. It was a painful process to undo bad habits. I intend to create good habits in my children from the beginning."

"Come Clean" Quiz

Have all of the family take this self-test and compute their score. Then have them take it again after you've had a chance to put some of the principles in this book into practice, and see the change.

Circle the number by the answer that applies to you:

	Never	Sometimes	When I'm Asked	Always
I make my own bed.	1	2	3	4
I put my dirty clothes in the hamper.	1	2	3	4
I hang up clothes that are still clean.	1	2	3	4
I clean the sink after brushing my teeth/mirror after flossing.	1	2	3	4
After I bathe, I clean off any tub ring.	1	2	3	4
My desk at school, home, or work is neat and clean.	1	2	3	4
I take my turn doing the dishes.	1	2	3	4
I mop or wipe up anything I spill.	1	2	3	4
I put my shoes and boots where they belong after I take them off.	1	2	3	4
My toys and collections are neat and organized.	1	2	3	4
I clean my own room and help with the rest of the house.	1	2	3	4

Scoring

12-18	19-24	25-36	37-48
Slob City	Dirty Bird	Keep it up	You deserve a new Corvette!

Chapter 3
Declutter First

We all know that there is too much stuff around the house, resulting in too much time spent shuffling it around and maintaining it, too much money spent, and too many arguments (on the way to Wal-Mart or the mall, and when we get back). Cutting back on junk and clutter is almost alone the solution for housework overload we are seeking. In fact, if you would just do something about all of those things no one really wants or needs, you could probably skip most of the rest of this book. If the stuff isn't there, no one has to clean it, clean around it, or organize it!

Thanks to availability, convenience, and ingenious new ways of financing, all of us, including the kids, have a mass of possessions that was unimaginable even in the 1950s or 1960s, let alone in pioneer days. Even the kids have tons more space and pushbutton ways to fill it and, sad to say, mostly pushover parents to pay for it.

You cannot cure a condition until you find and deal with the cause. When it comes to clutter, you can remodel rooms, expand drawers and closets, add two more bays to the garage, invest in every conceivable plastic container, and creatively label every last morsel of it, but that "too much" will still be there. Even if you have a place to put it, "too much" can still bury the family.

There is an easy answer here. Prevent and control the intake and inventory of excess, and your need for help around the house will be greatly reduced. This costs nothing to do; in fact, it will save you money.

> "One thing I am still working on is dejunking. It's hard to see what the kids need to put away if the house is full of stuff. There doesn't seem to be any point to putting a game away if the living room is full of sewing projects, books, magazines, shoes, coats, birthday gifts that never found a place, snack plates, and mail."

The Children Are an Easy Cure; You're Not

We, the adults, are the root of the problem here. Until children are about nine or ten years old, they don't really have much control over the amount of clutter they have. Just about everything they have comes from us. We control their surroundings; we are the landlord and superintendent of their lodgings and their things. We are master of the house. We determine what and how much there is and where it stays!

In my dejunking seminar presentations, as I'm heaping on the guilt about all of the junk in the average home, I make the statement, "and your children have 75 percent more toys than they need." That always gets an instant affirmative head nodding from the crowd. Even relieved looks of, "See, Don, it isn't just me," until I say, "Yes, folks, and you know why? *You gave them all that!*"

In the spirit of "Be good and I will bring you home/buy you some junk," millions of parents each day heap on little Brandon and Brittany some of the most worthless stuff imaginable. The undivided attention that we give our kids, according to a recent study at the University of Detroit, is on the average fifteen minutes a day, and only about two of those minutes are meaningful communication. Parents who seldom spend the time they want with a child often pick up a toy or gadget to replace themselves.

Working parents with guilty consciences, especially, often engulf their kids in all sorts of things, raising the clutter high-water mark to a record level in no time. We give kids things to compensate, regulate, and sedate them. Kids get even more gifts and things at divorce time or when parents are having trouble parenting. Even a fast-food trip has now become a fast way to getting more junk!

The kids are at a real disadvantage when it comes to dejunking their rooms. The only example they have is ours. They've watched us getting stuff and stacking it on the shelf and under the bed, and when the drawers and containers (and garage and storage shed) are full, they've gone with us to get more drawers and containers! We've even reprimanded them for using perfectly good junk storage boxes to make pirate ships and hideouts!

We warn our children about matches, the pool or nearby river, germs, strangers, crossing the street, drugs, pornography, but never about the harm, the danger, of the *stuff* that teaches us greed, warps our personality, insulates our sensitivities, and steals our time and money.

Today the majority of we parents are junk-a-holics who buy (and end up having to tend) too much stuff, showing our kids how to do the same. Control of our children starts with control of ourselves. If we want them clutter-free, guess who has to live that way?

You are the one who gave your kids most of this stuff, or encouraged them to collect it. You are also the parent, so you have the legal and moral right to reduce it, too! Most of us would agree on the following:

1. Kids actually need very little to be happy.
2. Big clutterfests aren't necessary for every event in their lives. (For instance, they don't need a major birthday party every year.)
3. The less there is to scatter, the less gets scattered. How many kids have you met, in this thing-loaded society of ours, who have been ruined for life by not having enough luxuries like fancy toys and video games? We all know scores who are spoiled and ungrateful because they have too much.
4. Kids are better than us at keeping memories without a whole shelf of mementos.

Another interesting twist here is that in the process of helping the kids declutter, we adults get a new view of and are more likely do something about our own clutter, so everyone wins in this situation.

PG (Parental Guidance) Dejunking

Here are a few pointers just to get you going. When it comes to the actual pruning or thinning, just remember that regardless of a person's age, there is some honor of ownership, and as soon as children are old enough to speak, they should have something to say as to exactly what has to go. Forty years later, there are kids who still haven't forgiven their parents for those "toss time" invasions on their stuff, after finding their old doll or train set in the garbage. What might look like clutter to you might be very precious to your child. For the sake of future relationships (and a great chance to teach the concept of decluttering to our kids), dejunking should be a team effort, with you coaching and your kids calling the shots. A few sneaky confiscation raids might have merit, but if you choose what they lose, they also lose the experience of dealing with their own problems. If not now, when and where do they learn?

> "The skill my daughter (who is now a young mother herself) lacks most is the skill of organization. That is my fault, I believe. When she was young I would organize her room for her–a place for everything and everything in its place. The problem was that I did it all for her, so she never learned how."

Give each child his or her own personal storage area—a box, shelf, whatever. When it overflows, have *the child* choose what should go. Kids' interests change, and only they know when something has ceased to be a fascination. Kids soon forget what's gone if you let them make the decisions and choose. And they usually choose better than we do.

Dejunking can even be an exercise in compassion. Kids will surprise you with what they will surrender to a friend or less fortunate kids. You could also offer to let them include some of their outgrown treasures in your next garage sale and let them keep the proceeds.

"The way I declutter is to ask my children to choose their favorite five (or whatever) toys and they go back in the boxes. Sometimes if the other toys are a bit painful to part with, they overcome this by selling them to me and I sell them on the equivalent of eBay and they get to buy a toy they want or even better an outing, no storing."

"I'm the mother of ten children and we live in a small rental house. Decluttering is a critical mission every day here, but it's difficult for young children to decide what to keep and what to give away. I knew they could do better so I brought out a bag of chocolate-covered peanuts. I promised one peanut for every donation item bigger than my hand. Within thirty minutes, my bag of peanuts was empty (and I was writing IOUs), my king-size bed was nearly hidden under donation items, and my children's bedrooms were much neater! My four-year-old beamed and said, 'If I don't like something more than a peanut, I just give it away!'"

One mother reported, "The hardest dejunking came in my son's room. I couldn't face doing it myself, so I gave him a huge box and told him to fill it with toys he no longer wanted. Ones that were broken or had pieces missing he could put in the large garbage can also in his room. I had to bite my tongue several times while he threw *my* favorite toys in the box. When he was finished, we took his box to his preschool and donated them to his class. The teacher was so thrilled to have some new toys for the class so she treated us to ice cream and also wrote me a check for a million thanks! Now my son can keep his room straight all the time, and keep his favorite toys at easy grasp."

Kiddie Clutter Cures

- Get rid of the stuff you saved for them! Most of this they would never want. I'd flush this away first . . . and fast!
- Practice regular rotation, but make sure no kids are around when you do it, because like us they will automatically cling to anything you take. Gather up the playthings that have fallen out of favor and box those babies and pack or hide them away for the next generation, or at least the next couple months.
- Exert some control over the total number of toys and possessions. As one of my readers put it, "Those that are tossed over their shoulders in search of the good stuff should be disposed of."

"I have found that the less toys children have, the better they play (alone, with each other, and when friends visit)."

"A good rule of thumb is to limit the number of toys they can have out. One is a good idea (if it is a set they can play with the whole thing), and they have to put that away before they get another one out. You would be amazed how much easier it is to clean if the clutter or mess is kept to a minimum."

"I've noticed that my son has lots of toys, but often the thing he wants most to play with is quite simple—for instance, he loves Daddy's measuring tape."

- Make sure all the things you give your kids or let them have is quality stuff. "Fewer but better" is the goal here. Get rid of the old rationale of free agency—that is, that they can buy or do what they want with their money. (Do you really think a ten-year-old with $40 from Grandma is just flooded with wisdom amidst all that is available?)

- Many parents have semiannual kid dejunking days: before birthdays, and before Christmas, to clear out the old, the broken, and the outgrown, and make way for the new.

- To raise children's awareness of clutter, have a show-and-tell contest. Have the kids line up and show off some things they found in their room or backpack—things with no value that they've been keeping forever. This will raise kids' awareness of owning, toting, and buying junk. Have Dad/Mom judge the worst junk, or all vote to decide it. This will make a big impression and is really a hoot.

- When your child's room gets overrun with junk, take the time to clean it out with him or her. While the two of you are sorting through and eliminating things that are broken or no longer of interest, try to remember what these things cost and help the child decide whether they were worth it. This may slow down the collection of other expensive, worthless things in the future.

- One big key to reducing clutter is making it easy to put things away. Make sure you give them a place. Many of us don't stop to think that a kid's room has to be his or her whole house. We only allow them one room, so it's really a combined sleeping and recreation area, living room, hobby shop, dining room, and storage area—

no wonder it's cluttered! Make sure they have space and a clearly defined place to store it all—toys, clothes, games, and books, computer stuff, and arts and crafts supplies.

- From my daughter Laura: "We have a shelf for each child in the main part of the house, near the kitchen. This is 'their shelf,' and they know it. When I find something of theirs around the house I don't run it to their room or yell at them, I just put it on their shelf. When they lose something they know to go to their shelf first—it's often there. When they come in from school they put their homework, shoes, and so on, there. This has eliminated tons of clutter, and hours of hunting and distress over lost items. Once every few weeks we clean the shelf to the bone, throwing away useless things and putting away the rest."

- Bear in mind that more space in a house or a child's room doesn't necessarily mean better organization and easier storage and cleaning. The proven law of packrattery is that "Stuff will accumulate in proportion to the space available."

- To make clutter control easier, and reduce the need for constant cleanup, keep a laundry basket or big plastic bucket handy in each room for quick cleanup. If possible, have one room designated as a playroom that does not always need to be perfectly tidy.

"If you have young children and you have the space, designate an area for a playroom and keep toys out of the bedroom. Allow only books in their bedrooms and one favorite stuffed toy, rotating if necessary."

"When something is outgrown, move it out. Tools and accessories for a nine-month-old are of no use in a three-year-old's environment. Yet even after the baby's off the bottle or out of diapers, etc., you'll find clothes, shoes, toys, tools, and utensils from a bygone era still around. And in the way creating unneeded thrashing, mix-ups, and hunting. The minute something has outgrown its usefulness, clean it . . . and store it for the next round. If there's not going to be a next time, pass it on. There's nothing more treasured and appreciated by a young family."—Mary Pride, author of *A Complete Guide to Getting Started in Homeschooling*

A Few Storage Ideas Now

Toys in general: Put a toy box in every major play area, such as each kid's room and the family room. You can even use something that matches the décor in nonkid rooms, but if you do make sure it's fitted with special (safety) toy-box hinges, or is lidless.

Stuffed animals: Nets (such as the Pet Net or Teddy Bed that you hang across the corner of a room do a good job of getting these hard-to-stack critters up and out of the way. If your child doesn't really play with stuffed animals or care much about them, you could consider just getting rid of most of them.

Multipart playthings: Store sets in clear plastic containers or plastic dishpans on shelves, one for each set.

Bathroom toys: A zippered net lingerie bag is great, with a suction cup on a hook stuck right through it. Or you can hang the bag on the faucet or showerhead.

Children's hair accessories: This trick is also good for any tiny things with great clutter potential. Try little plastic chests with divided drawers, or a fishing tackle box or the like.

Schoolwork clutter: We can't just throw it all away; it's their precious handiwork. But if you let those papers just pile up or try to keep them all, you'll soon be buried. Get a large plastic container for each child, and put his or her name on it. As those school papers, projects, report cards, and so on flow back from school, winnow them down to the best, most important, or interesting ones, and put them in the child's container. When the child grows up, give his container to him (after removing the dozen or whatever things that are most precious to you), so he can save what he still wants.

Books: Built-in bookcases with shelves divided into narrow (about twelve-inch) sections are best for holding up those skinny kid's books. These are far better than bookends, which are forever falling over.

Art supplies: Crayons, markers, brushes, scissors, and so on all fit neatly and compactly into one of those lazy-Susan-like artist's bins available at art-supply stores.

> "Our refrigerator was decorated for years with all the artwork and special papers our children brought home from school. We couldn't keep everything, of course, so we changed the display weekly. The most special items were kept in a big Rubbermaid container. I didn't want to throw the other pictures away, so I would have the child send the artwork to a relative or friend. They loved being able to mail the special 'letter,' and they loved the acknowledgment they got from the recipient of their artistic endeavors. Sometimes we would use large pieces of art as wrapping paper for a gift for a friend."

"What worked for me as a kid (I don't have my own yet) was having cleaning tools and storage items be my 'toys.' Walking around the major storage stores (like The Container Store) is a lot like walking around Toys R Us, except your parents WANT you to pick things! Picking out a coordinated system of bins for my stuff, shelves, and so on for my books, made me enjoy putting things in their places."

"One son collected baseball cards, so we bought him organizers to keep them in. The other son collected Matchbox cars, so we bought him organizers for those. Our daughter collected Barbie horses, so she had a special shelf to arrange them all on. I think acknowledging a child's special interests and giving them their own appropriate places to store their own things helps them to develop organizational skills."

Reducing Future Clutter

Here is a list to help you recognize what mostly ends up as clutter:

- Cheap junky electronic toys (watches, calculators, radios)
- Automated toys with broken or missing parts
- Cards of any kind—once opened they end up all over
- Anything based on the latest television or movie character (toys, games, models, clothes, accessories)—fads and frenzies of acquisition change fast here
- Broken or wrapperless crayons
- Duplicates (there are three ball mitts to keep track of now, for example, though only one can be used at a time)
- Fast-food meals that contain a toy (that kids collect and soon tire of)
- Stickers

- Little statues or figurines
- Junk bunkers (elaborate toy "organizing" boxes or shelves, Matchbox vehicle parking garages in which nothing is ever parked, and other such things tend to just collect and harbor more junk, or become clutter themselves)
- Prizes and giveaways (from stores, birthday parties, fairs, circuses, trips to the zoo, and the like)
- Half-completed paper projects, such as half-used coloring books
- Big stuff (such as tricycles and motorbikes) kept in kids' rooms. Don't store large things, outdoor equipment, or seldom-used stuff inside. Take it to the garage—have a place in the garage for their stuff too, such as sports equipment. Otherwise kids use equipment like this for a short season and then it remains in their room kicking around, taking up room for the next nine months.

Cut the Source!

"Our house is small, and one of the ways we control clutter is by not purchasing anything without knowing where in the house it will live. The kids, too, must be able to tell us where they will keep it before they buy anything new for themselves."

"I remind my children that the fewer possessions we have, the more time we have to spend together. When we go shopping and see impulse shopping about to happen, we say 'knicky knack' to remind each other."

A Few Last Pointers Now

First, don't make this a big marathon or crusade of purging everything all at once. Rome wasn't built in a day, and rooms or homes aren't decluttered in a day either. It took a while to accumulate and might take another while to undo, to disconnect some of the old clutter circuits and tear out some of the old mental wiring of always wanting and keeping more.

Second, dismiss the "bigger bag" or "bigger house" solution.

Don't get caught up in becoming a clutter storage expert with magnificent hangers, racks, storage bins, labels, drawers, and ever-bigger closets and garages. There is a better and simpler principle here—if you don't have the material, you won't have the mess. We all use too much creativity hiding and controlling what we should have cast away. How often do we see a mother pushing a cart full of plastic storage bins with a "going to get organized" look in her eyes, and three kids and a husband pushing carts loaded with junk right behind her?

Third, don't let the fact that clutter is presently well contained let you think it is fully conquered.

Fourth, don't get cold feet or the guilty willies when you are knee deep in garbage, junk, and clutter executions. Just remember how the kids love and have fun in a motel room or camp where the surroundings and available toys are sparse indeed. Plenty of excitement in life there!

Fifth, for inspiration and guidance in dejunking for the adults of the household, see *Clutter's Last Stand, Weekend Makeover,* or *For Packrats Only.*

> "How do we get kids to declutter? This one is easy for me! I had my teenagers read your books! Before my oldest daughter had even completed the second chapter of *Clutter's Last Stand*, she was cleaning the dreaded closets, kitchen shelves, and storage rooms in our home! We finally got together and used each other as motivators. I'd sip my coffee and she'd read me a chapter. We'd both be motivated and ready to go take on the day . . . until the next coffee break. Hey! Those sessions can be grueling and emotionally challenging!"

In closing, let me remind you that the first and most important step in cutting clutter is to cut the source. Your cleaning time, family fights, and arguments, and credit card statement chills will be reduced proportionately as the junk and "too much" are eliminated.

> "Don't be surprised by how often a home must be decluttered. We cannot ask our children to clean the floor or do the dishes if clutter is obscuring the floor or the sink!"

Chapter 4
Design Housework Out

Help doesn't have to come only from other humans or technology; it can come from the very structure and furnishings of your home.

Houses Are to Live In, Not For

We have three basic purposes when building or buying a home:

1. Shelter
2. Show
3. Appreciation (to gain net worth)

Then, in our general thrust to make living better, we begin to decorate the place, make it attractive, and fill it with furnishings and accessories. Somewhere along the line, sadly, we begin to live *for* the house instead of in it. In these three reasons to build a home or buy one, we need to replace number two. Instead of show, we should say *share*. The primary function of a home after shelter should be to share it—first with family and then with other relatives, friends, and neighbors. But we do most of our building, furnishing, and decorating for other adults to see and swoon over. (Just look at any of the many "beautiful house" magazines and books if you have any doubt about this.) But who really uses and most benefits from a home? The children. After a certain number of years, we adults begin to just exist there. We sink into the same old routines, concentrating more on our home's upkeep, its increase in value, and ability to improve our image. While we are doing all this, the children and their friends are running, jumping, poking, rolling, squabbling, playing, collecting, eating, and doing an endless number of other activities within the walls of the home.

From their rooms on out, children use a house harder and more often than most of the rest of us. Kids are also our number-one concern and expense, so doesn't it make sense to design their environment for them—in other words, to build in education, safety, durability, entertainment, and most of all, easy maintenance? This means building opportunities for abuse, litter, and breakage out—"kidproofing," as they say. How? Here is a personal example that not only explains it well but worked well!

While my wife and I were raising our own six children (and entertaining about half of the other kids in the neighborhood at our house much of the time), we found ourselves building our first home. It was near the finish point and we were standing in the empty bedroom intended for our two boys, reviewing its possible furnishing. Instead of wondering where we might locate the usual kids' room furniture, we joked about making the floor a large trampoline, maybe adding a drain in the middle of the floor for easy wash-down, a couple of jungle hammocks for beds, and a duffle bag hanger instead of a closet. We knew from our own childhood and all of the cousins we grew up with, too, that a lot of stuff ends up on the floor in a child's room no matter how big the dressers are. The boys were going to jump and roll and wrestle and kick the walls, pin and stick stuff to them (posters, awards, rubber spiders, and trophies). Hobbies would a find home here, too.

Suddenly one of us said, "We ought to build a stagecoach in here!" That got a laugh, but since we didn't have any furniture yet, it also got us thinking. Sure, why not. A stagecoach has storage—a top to store luggage and fight off the stage robbers, and a trunk in the back for dirty clothes. Inside the coach could be more storage. We could attach beds to both ends of the coach, built to the floor, with drawers under them, and we'd have eliminated the kicked-under-the-bed collection of lost shoes and socks, dirty clothes, sandwich crusts, and stray toys. We'd put a clothes closet inside the doors of the stage and the rear luggage box could be the dirty clothes hamper. We'd carpet the top of the coach for wrestling and jumping down onto the beds. We decided the driver's seat could be a smooth stair riser, and "the gold box" could be used for storing ball mitts, bats, etc.

By ten that night we had an actual plan for a combined storage and sleeping area. With some ¾-inch plywood and a saber saw, we made the shapes needed for the coach, nailed and glued them together, and added some fake wheels. It was simple to build. Barbara then ordered some custom-sized foam mattresses, and the boys were in paradise for the next ten years. That bedroom was built for use, required little cleaning, and looked good, too. There wasn't one leg or cabinet to clean around, or underside to collect dust and clutter. As long as we had it, the stagecoach room provided fun, comfort, and plenty of room for the imagination. And it cost very little.

When the boys were older we tore out the coach (in just a couple of hours) and put regular beds in there. Everything else in the room was wall mounted, rustic enough to get beat up a bit, and provided places for the things that we wanted kids to do. The only thing we didn't do (and we still regret it) was slant the closet floor, so nothing could be stacked in there and any junk would roll out and be underfoot so it would have to be picked up.

Was it a good idea? The answer is that it was a good idea for *us*. You have your own individual considerations—the number and ages of your kids, their interests, and the size and shape of the bedroom space available. We could also have considered a space vehicle, or a racecar with storage under the hood and in the trunk. Or we could have erected a skyscraper with storage drawers up the front that looked like windows and side openings to hold toys.

It's amazing what a simple structure like the stagecoach can do to reduce the headaches in kid territory. Not only did the coach provide a great place for our kids to play growing up, it housed clean and dirty clothes and toys, provided a sleeping area, and kept the room from ever getting cluttered enough to require a major cleaning operation.

Preventative Design

Preventative design simply means designing to reduce cleaning and maintenance. If something doesn't get dirtied or torn up, it won't need to be cleaned up.

You don't have to undertake a major building project to take advantage of preventative design. The majority of what we are cleaning and maintaining in a house is things like floor and wall coverings, window coverings, fixtures, and furniture—items that wear out over time and have to be replaced. By making some low-maintenance choices the next time you change these things, you can cut out considerable cleaning. The whole thrust here is to eliminate the need to police, fix, or clean. Design can do it!

Don't overlook design's ability to give you the help you need to maintain both your family and the family dwelling.

Low-maintenance building is not a new idea. Women figured it out hundreds if not thousands of years ago, and only recently are builders and architects (who are mostly men) finally buying in. Now we are finally making some progress. Many of us have built low-maintenance houses, and they pay us dividends in more ways than money alone. Remember that using the principle of "deflection" is much easier than straining for perfection.

Many of us, after growing up and having kids of our own, remember things we'd have liked to have in our own rooms as a child. Or we imagine things we would like to build for our children now. Some of these ideas are pretty wild; others, you wonder why someone out there hasn't enacted already. Often when you enter a kid's room or some other area they have just decimated, or are cleaning up a mess they made and left behind, you hatch an idea or two of how and what you might do to avoid running into this situation again. This is right-on-target thinking—now you just need to get the nerve to do it. It usually takes more nerve than money to come up with something clever or unique that might prevent the mess in the first place.

Use your imagination! You were a kid once. Your brainstorms will pay off handsomely.

Some Maintenance-Freeing Moves

Use your own wisdom in the layout and decoration of your children's rooms—don't just copy what you see in the "glamour home" magazines. They have some good ideas for children's rooms and areas, but they often overdo it. Use your own imagination and experience with what makes messes! To start your own list of low-maintenance ideas, here are some design features that have worked well for me and other parents:

Built-ins: Earlier I mentioned the stagecoach we built in our sons' room. Besides being a great place to play, it had a built-in clothes closet, toy box, and hamper, as well as built-in beds with storage drawers underneath. This really reduced the places (like under the bed or behind things) to litter or

leave anything. In a later home we built inset places in the wall (instead of shelves sticking out) for hobbies, displays, posters, pinups, and collectibles. This kept them out of the line of fire. Audio and video equipment, desks, and computer workstations are excellent things to build in, too.

When furnishings are built in, they can't be disarranged or tipped over, and there are far fewer exposed edges and corners for kids to get hurt on.

Minimal sharp corners and edges: Many homes are, in effect, jungles of sharp points. All of these points and edges are right at kid level, and if a kid runs into them he'll have a cut forehead or blackened eye. The first two years of a child's life are spent learning to walk—falling, bumping, and grabbing at everything in his or her path. Tumbles are a part of the game. Besides avoiding sharp edges, be sure that furniture isn't loose or unstable and that it can't be pulled over. Avoid sharp-edged furniture or furniture with a lot of exposed wood or metal. Also, watch out for things that tempt children to climb. If there is a way to climb on it, children will try.

Hang It!: If there's anything you can get up off the floor, do it! When the place where something belongs is clearly established, easy to reach, and easy to use, it encourages kids to put things back rather than strew them around. Brackets,  hangers, clamps, pegboard, and the like can be easily anchored to most walls. You can even hang the trashcan on a wall bracket. It's easy to sweep or vacuum under, and it never gets tipped over. For that matter, why not wall-mount a small vacuum in there, too?

Semi-gloss or high-gloss paint: It's surprising how many people use flat paint or wallpaper in action places. Grease, oil, ink, and crayon then become hard or impossible to clean off. Use gloss enamel paint, so the bad stuff will bounce off or clean off easily. And use a high-quality brand, so you won't have to be repainting before the year is out. There are even extra stain-resistant and scrubbable paints specifically designed for children's rooms.

Durable, washable wall coverings: For the walls in a child's room, vinyl wall covering, hardwood paneling, or even carpet might be a better choice than painted wallboard. You'll have less dents and dings to repair. You don't have to put coverings like this all the way up the wall, since the bottom half is what gets the hardest use. These are very low maintenance, they look good, provide some sound-proofing, and are hard to ruin.

Vinyl flooring: Vinyl flooring (such as extra-soft cushioned vinyl) is better than carpet for young children and for any child's room that will be exposed not just to the usual spots and spills, but also to heavy craft activity. Toys roll better on vinyl anyway! You can always switch to carpet when children are older. Half vinyl and half carpet can be a good idea in a child's room, too. Use low-pile, tight-weave carpet when you do use carpet.

Camouflage: Yes, in the war on dirt, this is fair! The carpet and wall colors (and maybe even some of the furnishings) in a child's room should be capable of camouflaging dirt and disorder. This means they should match the potential fallout of food, drinks, pet hair, glue/clay/craft mess, makeup, and so on. A textured, multicolor carpet shows less soiling then a solid pastel. In a child eating area, consider colors like gravy brown,

butter yellow, spinach green, pizza red, and taco orange. Again, *houses are made to live in, not live for.* When decorating and choosing furnishings and accessories, do whatever you can to reduce the beating a place takes as well as the need to be constantly cleaning and straightening.

Lower closet rod: How many mothers tell kids and even toddlers to hang up clothes when the average clothes rod is fifty-five inches high or higher? Installing a lower rod will cost only a few dollars and save thousands of hours of time! When the kids grow up or move, you can remove or replace the rod in minutes. (Even in adult closets, low rods are handy for short clothing items.)

Low, well-labeled drawers: If you provide drawers for clothes or anything else that little ones can reach, and label them boldly and attractively, there'll be fewer pajamas, mittens, and T-shirts strewn around.

Oversized switchplates: This is an inexpensive little adjustment that cuts spot cleaning and wall damage. Oversize switchplates provide a larger surface area that is harder and tougher than wallboard to stand up to all the abuse this area gets.

Adequate waste receptacles: We see the saddest trash containers in kids' rooms—too small, easy to tip over, hard to dump into, hard to clean, and so on. Put a professional-quality plastic trash can in there.

One blanket, not three: Bed mess is inevitable. Smart parents use a single heavy blanket or comforter with a washable cover and one sheet instead of many layers of covers and spreads. It makes bed-making easy and encourages kids to do it.

A generous bulletin board: If the gallery for greeting cards, souvenirs, school papers, messages, calendars, and photos is nice enough, that's where kids will put this stuff instead of pinning and taping it all over the walls (damaging the surface, then falling off later). You can buy a nice big bulletin board and a white- or chalkboard for drawing. It's worth it!

A "pocket" shelf: Have you ever noticed there is no real place in a kid's room to put some of the most important items (and the stuff that always gets strewn): knapsacks, purses, book bags, duffel bags, and pocket contents? These things always end up on the floor or the already-crowded end table or dresser top, establishing a bad habit that carries on into adulthood. Design a generous-sized shelf with a lip so that pencils, marbles, and stray Tootsie Rolls won't fall onto the floor.

A desk of their own: While a desk is something most people don't get until they're in their twenties, most of us need one (if not two) all our lives! Kids need one, too—a place to write, draw, color, and put private stuff. The inside of a child's desk might get a little junky, but all those papers, pencils, rulers, and markers will be off the floors, walls, and out of your kitchen drawers. If I could do it over, I'd have bought all my kids a desk. It confines the action and the mess.

Why not alter or designate a room in your house *for kids only*? You don't necessarily have to make any structural alterations. Just assemble some attractive toys, games, and maybe a television and computer, and WOW! Your home will be a favorite spot for your children and their friends. If you have one room (the larger the better) just for a playroom where the children go to play, the rest of the house (all of the other rooms) will not be messed up or damaged as often. Figure out some ways to confine messy activities to places that can take it so they can be enjoyed without adding to the burden of housework. We made a bright little kid-sized doorway leading into a delightful playroom for the grandkids. What kid can resist an open door? It worked! They climb into that room and play for hours. They have fun and don't make messes, break anything, or get into things they shouldn't in the rest of the house. Small children aren't the only cause of mess and damage—older kids, teenagers, and adults also generate plenty of clutter in the process of entertaining themselves. But if you design, build, and organize for vigorous or messy kids' activities, giving them their own place, the cleaning and maintenance of the house as a whole will be reduced immensely.

Personally I like to eliminate doors, drawers, and anything else that has to be constantly opened and closed. I will never have doors on a closet—all of ours are walk-in, and I believe in "total exposure" (being able to see where things are and where they go). Other people like things concealed. Let's not think inside the box here (inside the kids' rooms or the house only). For example, let's take the garage. A little money spent on finishing and painting the walls and sealing the concrete floor into a shining, easy-to-clean surface can make the garage an inviting place for projects that can easily ruin the counters and floor of the kitchen or elsewhere. You can shift activities, encourage participation, and even leave things partly finished for a while here out of the main flow of traffic. Think prevention rather than restoration!

Think outside the box (and the closet)

Here are some way-out ideas for a maintenance-freeing child's room design to get you thinking:

- A drawerless room.
- A no-fold clothes storage system.
- A portable closet.
- Wall dispenser with three or four essentials.
- Buzzer for reminders.
- A no-make bed.
- Innovative under-bed storage.

- Magnetic strips in clothes that attach to magnet wall strip so kids can throw clothes to wall rather than to floor. You could even make the walls themselves magnetic—with studs that are magnetic, electrical plate covers, or chair rails, or whatever! Then there would be extra "closet" space off the floor. What better use for walls?
- Scissor gear (retractable, spring-loaded) mounted on the ceiling, so kids can pull down necessities. Or how about making the entire ceiling a giant magnet? You take off your clothes, toss them upward, and they catch and hang down just far enough to be grabbed the next time but are out of your face. This would provide not just automatic airing out and instant decoration, but a clean floor.
- Shoe sensor for lost shoes.
- "Ferris wheel" rotating shoe rack that stores shoes and delivers them easily in pairs. This could be situated parallel to the wall so it doesn't take up much space.
- Corner "garages" for toys or dirty clothes, a corner shoe garage, or corner basketball-hoop clothes hamper with wheels.
- On/off light sensors, kid style.
- Between-stud furniture inserts (like the fold-out ironing boards) that can be folded back up after use.
- Closet organizers or adapters for children (plenty of adult ones out there).
- Wall hung/mounted office unit (with suspended chair) that slides in under a counter.
- A dirty-clothes chute that speed-delivers clothes to the laundry room.
- An odor-neutralizer spray that activates every time a light goes on (to get rid of kid-room smells).
- In-room "brag" wall, for measuring height and hanging mementoes and awards.
- Sensor door lock that won't release until room is in order.

A great architect once said, "Beauty is in the promise of function." That means a big ugly nail hanging from the ceiling is beautiful if it hangs an airplane for a child (so it isn't on the floor getting trampled).

I hope some of these ideas trigger new ideas of your own. At the least, this kind of brainstorming should convince you that something can be done and that it will make a difference in the amount of housework that needs to be done every day and week.

Invite Them Outside

Let's not forget the exterior area of a home, which kids enjoy much more than most adults do.

The whole idea of *having* is *using*. Don't keep a yard only for display; the more time people spend outside, the less clutter, spilt food, and abuse the inside of the house will get. Most of us need to spend more time outside anyway.

If you had the chance to sit and read on a bench in the fresh air, would you choose a stuffy living room? If there are ropes on the trees and swing sets outside, the kids are less likely to be swinging on the drapes inside. If you make the outside of your house inviting, a lot of playing, eating, visiting, and projects will be done out there. When my friend Sandra Phillips built her low-maintenance home, she even modified the chimney so that her teenagers and their friends could use it as a sport-climbing wall.

Yard Furniture

When you consider how often you have to replace it, flimsy, collapsible outdoor furniture isn't as inexpensive as it seems. Furniture that needs reweaving or regular repainting

to prevent rust is one more chore you'd happily chuck if you could. And who feels like running outside at the first sign of rain to throw a plastic cover over everything? You want *permanent* furniture that can stand up to the weather outside—tables, chairs, benches, garbage cans, everything. Wooden picnic tables and benches are good if you move a lot, but if you have roots down, why not build things to stay? The initial cost is only slightly higher, and the furniture will last forever. For ideas, look at what public parks and rest areas use, such as furniture of concrete and heavy galvanized steel. Sturdy plastic furniture is another good choice.

Built-In Recreation

I'm not suggesting that you convert your home into a public recreation facility, but if you can't flex your physical and mental muscles at home, where can you? By building in recreation, I don't mean that you have to install heated swimming pools, tennis courts, or horse trails—the simple things are usually the most used and enjoyed. Some of the most fun things call for the simplest equipment.

You know the things your family really enjoys—pick two or three of your favorites, and build for those things. Don't overdo it, or you'll end up having too much to take care of. You want to avoid building in equipment for short-lived enthusiasms and concentrate on pastimes that have stood the test of time.

Here are some easy ways to make your yard a place to remember. A few simple graphics and some equipment can turn part of your yard or driveway into an activity center for volleyball, basketball, badminton, or whatever. Your local sporting goods store should have instructions for the official layouts for all ball courts; if not, have the kids get them from their coaches. Lines are easy to apply (using striping paint for asphalt or concrete), especially if you put down tape to guide you. All you need for a ball-and-Frisbee area is a wide-open expanse of lawn or blacktop—with no obstructions to trip over and neighbors' windows safely out of range.

There is no way this book or, for that matter, an architect with twelve kids and a brilliant mind can cover all the possibilities of design that can and will reduce, prevent, or eliminate care and cleaning on the home front. Our needs and creativity, ever-improving technology, and the good old profit motive will keep on producing new ideas. My point, I hope made strongly, is that you have the liberty and probably the means to come up with and do things to fit your own needs as well as those of your children, your mate, and other family members such as aged parents. You can build these things into your home's structures and furnishings. Even if your ideas are strikingly different or a little off the deep end, don't let that stop you from investigating and eventually enacting the best of them.

Chapter 5

Introducing the Idea: Getting Everyone to Buy In

"My kids have never known life without chores. It's how families need to run ... everyone doing his or her part."

In an appearance on Philadelphia's *People Are Talking* television show, I once handed six members of the audience each a slice of bread and had them tear it in pieces and throw it on the floor in front of them. Then I had the host pick up everyone's discarded bread as fast as he could. It took him twenty-five seconds. Then I gave each of the same people another slice and had them tear it up and throw it down again. But this time I had each person pick up his own mess. It took less than five seconds.

This is the revelation you are going to be sharing with the family—housework will be much less of an issue if everyone helps. A clean house, clean clothes, and meals don't just happen—you must become a family team to *make* them happen.

A Few Words from the Cleaning Coach

The following is the speech I've often given youngsters during my visits to schools as a cleaning coach. You might find it helpful somehow in the cause.

Hi, I'm the Cleaning Coach. I like to clean so I much I do it for a living. I even carry a toilet suitcase! My cleaning career started on the farm. When things were messy and dirty it caused bad feelings and confusion. And when a chance to go fishing or play ball came, I'd miss it because I couldn't find my mitt or fishing pole. More than once, when I left my possessions on the floor or outside, they got ruined by the rain or tromped on. My drawers got so stuffed with junk they wouldn't close.

One day I decided to be a winner and keep everything clean. As I did this, my parents trusted me more, and my ball playing improved.

I went to college. No good jobs were available to help work my way through, so I started my own cleaning company and became the owner of a large national company by cleaning houses, toilets, and yards. Plus I had fun and made hundreds of friends. Many students, like you, worked for me and had great adventures in cleaning. I've done thousands and thousands of radio, television, and stage appearances, all about the importance of cleaning. Why? Because when you and your place are clean, you feel good. Try it—you'll like it.

Sad to say, most of the cleaning of our messes is done by mothers, maids, and janitors. If mothers spend most of their time cleaning up our messes, we have cheated them out of a portion of their lives. Would you cheat your mom?

You can do it—you can clean! You are big enough, strong enough, and smart enough to take responsibility for your own messes, like so:

DON'T WAIT TO BE TOLD OR ASKED. Your sharp young eyes can see mess anywhere and dirt can't hide from you. And litter just lies there waiting for your hands, which are faster and more limber than anyone's! So volunteer. Yes! Jump right in and pick up things and clean them off, organize them. When you start doing this, you're one step toward greatness.

YOU CAN DO IT ALL! People often say kids are too little or too inexperienced to clean, but you know better. You can clean anything as well and as fast (even faster) than the big people. A sturdy stepstool makes you instantly tall, vacuums adjust to any height, and when you're small you can often get into places the giants can't.

YOU'LL BE BUILDING YOUR MUSCLES/BODY, TOO. Cleaning, with all of the bending, reaching, lifting, climbing, and carrying involved in it, will help you become strong, and quick, too. Cleaning builds brain muscles as well.

One good way to unveil all of this is to hold a family meeting at a time when everyone is in a good mood, or at least calm and relaxed.

> "My sons never, and I mean NEVER, balked at my requests for household help and I think it is because I started them when they were young and always let them know how crucial their help was to the smooth running of the household since both my husband and I have always worked full-time."

> **"I think communicating about chores is one key to the cooperation I get from my kids."**

> "One thing that has helped a lot is having a family motto. It goes like this, 'We are a FAMILY, we work TOGETHER' with those important words emphasized. We all have special jobs but everyone pitches in when we need it because 'We are a FAMILY, we work TOGETHER.'"

The Teaching Moment

Presenting the case for help around the house is one thing; getting the rest of the family to buy into it quite another. But buying in is essential, and accomplishing this is your real mission here. The ideal way to do this is to pick just the right moment.

My mother was a master of timing. She knew precisely when to seize a moment of disagreement or discouragement to teach a principle that would stick with you forever.

I remember the hottest Idaho day of my young life. I was thirteen, and I'd been lollygagging, griping, and groaning out in the garden, making my mother force me to pull every weed. She waited till I'd reached a complete standstill and then sat down and told me about a soldier she'd met while in the hospital once. He'd lost both legs in a land-mine explosion. This grown man sat there in his bed one day and wept for the opportunity to work in a garden, among the plants and flowers again. That really stunned me. I felt so sad for that soldier, and so lucky I could work, that I vowed from then on, no matter how I felt, I would never be lazy again. The rest of those rows were cleared of weeds mighty quick.

Likewise, my mother could have just given the old "don't drink or smoke" lecture to her kids anytime, but she was smarter than that. She always waited for "the moment," the best frame for something, before she laid it on us. I had a bad stomach virus once and was sick—vomiting, dizzy, nauseous to my very toe tips, looking forward to death as a release. As I was leaning over the toilet in agony I remember Mom putting her hand on my forehead and saying, "Donald, remember this is exactly how you feel after you drink alcohol." My brain cells quickly organized a "No way will I ever drink, then" commitment, and I've never had a twinge of desire for any form of booze since. All because of the masterful timing of a good mother!

One of my own teaching moments cropped up when I took a group of Scouts to Philmont, in the mountains of New Mexico. We packed in and camped where no roads existed. There were twelve of us, and everyone's turn to cook and wash dishes came once every three days. After six days out the Scouts were really grumbling. One of them threw his mess kit on the ground and said, "This sucks—we came here to have fun and we have to spend three hours a day [every three days, remember] doing all this." They all agreed and were disgusted and really put out by having to do all of this "housework." "Lay your plates and spoons down a minute, boys," I said.

I asked them all to sit there for five minutes and think about something. "You are all complaining about this tiny bit of camp housework you have to do just a couple of days this whole year, while having a grand time on all the rest of this trip. Your mothers (or other caregivers) have done this three

times a day for every day of your fifteen years of life. That's
16,200 times it has been done for you and you are upset about
doing it a few times during one week of one year. It is your
food and *your* mess."

They were stunned. They had never thought before about
who did all of this work in their behalf. Eleven boys were
changed when they went home—those mothers and fathers
made a good investment in that Scout camp.

> "While they are very little (or any age), watch for and seize
> the moment. Our son at age five looked on wide-eyed as I
> did the laundry, and asked, 'Can I do that?' 'Sure!' I replied
> and showed him how. I watched and coached him through
> his first load starting that very moment. He has done his
> own laundry ever since."

A Great Tool of Leadership: Expectation

Expectation is a way of including others in the responsibility
and rewards of home care and upkeep as well as just the work
itself. It is providing the time and space and chance for others
to buy into the deal. It is putting trust and confidence in other
hands and minds besides yours.

There is a strong impulse in people, especially children,
to respond to and do what is expected. You can list and assign
all day and night, but that is only the mechanics of the matter.
Action comes from being motivated, having a common cause,
something they know is worthwhile and that you expect them
to reach.

Expectation is an effective way to harness people's pride
productively, and it may even tap into the powerful force
called competitiveness. We humans live to reach goals and
show accomplishment, and when we know someone who
loves us or is paying us is expecting something, we will take
ownership of it. There are numerous ways to get people to "do

their duty." We often coerce or coax action or productivity out of people. But look around and look at yourself—we respond much better to expectation.

Expectation transfers responsibility into other people's arena, bounces the ball into their court. Notice the difference when someone invites you to something—how you react when it is an optional decision. But as soon as they add, "We really need you to be there," you suddenly assume a much higher degree of ownership of the event at hand. The coach might say, "Well, George, play your best," but if he's smart, he'll say, "George, I expect you to score twenty points and outrun any man guarding you." Now George is playing to expectations, not just assignment.

The opposite is nearly crushing, such as when someone says to you, "You disappointed me." Those words hurt when they come from anyone, but they sting even more when someone you really care about says them. In other words, "You fell below my expectations!" People hate and dread falling below expectations. And when they are working to the expected, they figure more of the details out on their own. (That's because no one is holding their hand, only their heart and sense of self-esteem.) People will function at a medium level for pay or contractual agreements, but for expectation they become soldiers who will fight and die for their cause.

Orders like, "Have this room cleaned, the car washed, the clothes folded (or whatever) by the time I get back" rely on obedience. Saying "I know you will have the room clean, the car washed, and the clothes folded by the time I get back" puts the onus on them to please (along with a dose of the guilts) and shifts the task from an assignment to a duty. You of course must keep yourself in the position of a powerful expecter, someone who has authority and clout and someone they love and want to please.

"I have four children between the ages of three and eleven. They have become very good little helpers for the most part. The main way I've gotten them to help is quite simple: I've expected them to help, and they know that I expect them to."

"Children will rise to the standard that you set and expect of them. So Moms . . . set the standard!"

Why Clean?

Kids need reasons as much as adults do. Sustained productivity has to have a big element of spontaneous self-motivation—it won't just pour forth from programmed outlines. Once someone is sold on a cause, they understand the why of a thing—it makes all the difference.

Tie Cleaning in to What They Want to Be

Tying cleaning in to what young people want to be is a strong (and clean!) motivation. Kids are always asked the old question, "What do you want to be when you grow up?" There are many familiar answers: a pilot, nurse, president, executive, athlete. Now is the time to explain how being neat and clean carries over directly to being good at that job.  ("One of the first things you notice about pilots is how neat and clean they are.") A big influence on my decision to be clean in my own life was a single sentence of my mother's. We were cleaning some vegetables once and she stopped and said, "One of the first things that attracted me to your father was the way he always kept himself, his workplace, and his tool shop so clean!" That really registered because like most kids, I worshipped my father and wanted to be like him.

Point Out the Personal Benefits of "Clean"

It's okay to tell kids to do something because it "makes Mommy happy" or "makes Grandpa smile," but that's secondary to convincing them that their own actions can make things better and happier for themselves. Keep pointing out the personal benefits of clean:

"You'll feel better, in a clean room, clean shirt, or clean yard."

"You can find things easily."

"You'll have more room to play."

"You'll be less likely to get hurt, and you won't get sick as often."

"Your toys stay nicer when they are clean and neat."

"Your things will be much less likely to be broken, dirty, or lost."

"Everyone likes you more when you're clean."

"It's a good way to get a better allowance, or to earn extra money."

"Learning to clean is just part of basic training for life. When you grow up, you'll be ahead—you'll already know how!"

Some Thoughts from My Readers

"You are doing your children a favor by teaching them good habits. When they are older, they will be pleasant and desirable roommates. They will be welcome houseguests in other peoples' homes. They will appreciate the hard work that goes into keeping a place clean and well maintained. They will pitch in when it's time to clear the table, and this will earn them friendship and respect. These are management skills, job skills, relationship skills."

"We all know that having a good work ethic will be crucial to our kids when it is time to 'cut the apron strings' and send them on their way. Knowing how to work will undoubtedly help to ensure their success in the 'real world.'"

"Who wants to grow up and one day move into their first home not knowing how to take care of themselves and their apartment? Unless they have a doting mother that does their laundry till they get married (don't laugh, it's happened), or have a trust fund that allows them to hire a cook or housekeeper."

"Ask yourself why you want them to clean. For me, I want to teach them skills that will enrich their lives. I don't want them to have to spend their weekends doing backed-up cleaning when they can be doing more important things. I also want peace in our lives, and we can't have it when the house looks like a junkyard. I want my kids to know how good it feels to live in order."

Kids Want to Help

This may be one of the best-kept secrets of the modern world, but young people actually want to help. Polls and questionnaires that I and other authors have taken show that when given a chance to vote for helping, yea or nay, the majority of kids say they want to and should help. Consider the fact that children often compete to do jobs at school, and "play house" by themselves, with no encouragement from adults. In fact, if they weren't watching us grunt and groan over household chores, they might be very likely to think that cleaning was a great adventure.

"I own a hair salon and the youngsters who come in for haircuts have always been allowed to get the broom and sweep to their hearts' content. I can't think of many who failed to take me up on my offer. They love to sweep!"

Let Everyone in on the Costs

Here, let me propose a big step that very few of us have taken. When the question is raised, "Who is in overall charge of the house and its inhabitants and needs?," the answer is usually the parents. They are basically the ones paying for it all, so we let them be the central worrier about the sustaining of it all, too. Sharing this burden or load of the home's maintenance is a powerful move that refocuses this premise. Everyone should share the worry and weight of the upkeep of the entire facility.

Why not let people know what things really cost? Few children (and, sad to say, not all parents) really know what it costs to run a home. We work to take care of our families, always trying to bring a little more money in than goes out. Where and how it goes can be pretty elusive sometimes. Kids don't have a clue that they are part of the expenses; they think that things just take care of themselves. Even when we give kids the old money lecture ("We are about broke and cannot afford X,") we usually manage to come up with the money for X. I see grown kids, even in college, wasting food, leaving lights on, running through a whole washer and dryer cycle for one little garment, or showering for fifteen minutes, using tons of expensive hot water.

Kids live in and use the place, thinking it is just there. Kids come home from college or move back in with parents to save rent, because living at home is "free." Even with their degree or advanced degrees, they often have not a clue that it costs a household about $600 a month, even if there is a spare room, to keep an extra adult. As far as they're concerned, the food just appears magically on the table, and the newspapers, lights, washers and dryers, and telephones cost nothing and are just there for the taking or using. I think you can see where I'm going with this.

"I have noticed that children who help with work tend to use two irritating words much less: 'I'm bored.'"

The great conversion from *the* house to *our* house needs to take place. Why not start to teach the fundamentals of economics? You kids will end up years ahead of what is taught in college, and your spouse or mate will be wiser with the dollar. Now don't soften up and say, "I don't want my kids to worry about money—they're just kids." You can be sure that money will end up being one of the prime catalysts for arguments, divorces, and irritations in their lifetime. What better time and place to make people aware of what it costs to live? Someday, they will have a clue what all of this will cost them.

If everyone living in a house knew exactly what their share of the costs was, and in some way it came out of their funds, they would waste less and appreciate more. House costs are almost all consuming now; it often takes both parents to fund the cost of living. One of the most important things you can do in the process of getting help around the house is to educate everyone (yourself included) about the costs. It is one of the best educations a child can have; it is real arithmetic and an instiller of values.

Chart it out something like this, citing all costs as monthly and then daily:

Cost of Running a Household	Monthly	Daily
House payment (including interest)		
Real estate taxes		
House insurance		
Electricity		
Gas or oil, etc.		
Water		
Garbage removal		
Repairs		

Cost of Running a Household	Monthly	Daily
Improvements (new couch, refrigerator, rug, new paint)		
Phone		
Internet		
Groceries		
Medical and dental bills and insurance		
Cleaning supplies or services		
Clothes and linens		
Cosmetics and grooming		
Car payments, repairs, and gasoline		
Recreation/entertainment		
Total:		

When you get this done (and after the initial shock to even the adults) then assemble everyone and divide the total amount equally by three or six or however many are in your family. When the twelve-year-old finds it costs $1,000 a month or $35 every day or $3 an hour for him to live here, he will shift into different thinking. The same is true of mooching kids who live at home free of charge after age eighteen and any guests of theirs.

When someone knows what their room costs, it changes their perspective. When they know what is being paid for the hot water, the lights, the food, and the vacations, you have a foundation to use for *expectation*. Best of all, kids will leave home financially educated better than any course or school or ten bad money experiences could teach them. (You may consider confining this technique to children eight or nine and older, depending on the maturity level of your children.)

Giving someone the opportunity to buy into something and assume part ownership is almost magical. That all-important buy in, just like decluttering and designing, will save a lot of time, effort, and frustration. Motivated and responsible people seldom need nagging, and they seldom need to report in or be followed up on. They take charge and make it happen.

Have Some Good Answers Ready

Our efforts to recruit new helpers will generate some of the most creative pleading and good, logical excuses imaginable. Your recruits will hit you with these when you are too tired or befuddled to come up with a good answer. Here are a few examples:

"I don't have time."
"It's not my job."
"It doesn't look dirty to me."
"I just did it."
"I don't know how."
"It's boring."
"I'll do it later."
"I'll sue you for child abuse!"
"My friend Johnnie doesn't have to work around the house."

Kids can quickly come up with comparisons, and adults can, too. Have you ever heard a subtle jibe like, "George's wife heats up the plates before she serves dinner on them"? The people brought up in these examples are always good ones—we can't dispute that little Johnnie Junkroom is the most popular kid in school or that George's wife is outstanding. When these comparisons crop up, you better have a better answer than these:

"Look around, Clayton, do you see little Johnnie anywhere here?"
"Good for him. Now you get yourself in gear or no supper."
"Well then why don't you go live at her house?"

They'll even quote you against yourself, brilliantly! So think ahead and be ready. Maybe an answer along the lines that "This is our house and we all work around here, even your friends if they show up. You are luckier than they are, you've started college already, right at home." Or maybe even just a simple, "Let's go to it!"

Pages 54, 58-59, and 189-191 in this book will give you much of the ammunition you need when "excuses" crop up.

"Already, from my seven-year-old, I hear, 'But I was at school all day, why do I have to do X or Y?' Uggh!!!"

"Sometimes, I have my children time their tasks. This shows, for example, that making a bed takes approximately three minutes. Thus the excuse of not having time to do something usually isn't valid."

"If one of the kids should claim, 'That's not my chore!' I ask them how they think that response would fly with their dad's boss. Or if someone does a half-hearted job, I'll ask what the consequences would be if their dad gave that kind of effort at work."

"When you tell kids to clean up, and they say 'Why?' the answer 'Because I told you so' sometimes has to be enough."

Chapter 6

The Self-Cleaning Family: Everyone Cleans His or Her Own Mess

Seventy percent of housework is just clutter and litter control and dealing with the aftermath of eating, grooming, and dressing—the clothes we wear, and the food and paper we go through daily. That's why housework isn't a woman's or even a family's job but a personal, individual responsibility. If you can start by just getting each member of the family to take care of or minimize the mess he or she creates, the household load as a whole will be greatly reduced.

Cleaning our own mess gets down into the heart of responsibility. What could be more basic than putting back in order the things we disordered and removing the dirt we ourselves tracked in?

Remember all those times your mother said, "You kids treat strangers better than you do your own brothers and sisters!"—and we did. We do exactly the same thing in housework. While at another's place we will politely pick up our apple cores or break our necks to return the used lemonade glass to the sink, and often get up from a meal to offer, "May I help?" Four hours later at home, we haven't the slightest inclination toward any such action. All the things we do at the homes of others and away—let's just try to do the same at home.

The cure to the "housework" problem will come from one basic thing: each of us becoming aware and considerate enough to take care of our own junk and mess.

> "Many of the tasks home cleaners have to perform are really the result of bad manners. Someone has a glass of milk but doesn't wash the glass. Someone eats dinner but doesn't clear the dishes. Sometimes helping out is just a question of courtesy."—Congressman George Miller

"Kids need to be taught from an early age to take care of their personal things. They need to hang their coat on a hook rather than drop it on the floor. They can take off their shoes and put them neatly out of the main traffic area. They can put their dirty dishes in the sink from an early age. The sooner they learn that no one else is responsible to pick up after them, the better off they will be in the future."

"If there is toothpaste in the sink, show the child how to clean it up right away, as soon as they finish brushing their teeth."

"My biggest pet peeve is the toilet—how a perfectly cleaned bathroom will smell like urine in a day when the boys haven't watched where they're going. I keep saying 'Go IN the toilet, not on or around it . . .'"

Things Anyone Can Do to Reduce the Need for Cleaning

One of the most valuable things you can teach children—or adults for that matter—is how to catch and clean up their own fallout, whether it be cookie crumbs, candy wrappers, nutshells, empty pop cans, dropped sweatshirts, or scattered puzzle pieces. The fact that we do a giant project doesn't give us immunity from the cleanup: sawdust, drips of solder, wood chips, plaster dust, and so on. We don't have to leave a mess in plain view to advertise our accomplishments. What we actually did accomplish will be appreciated even more if it doesn't leave a big cleanup job behind.

Anyone who's done any backpacking or wilderness camping knows the rule there—"Anything you pack in has to be packed out." After a week up in the beautiful Primitive Area of Idaho when I was a boy, we flattened every can and along with anything else that couldn't be burned, brought it back out with us, and took it to the dump. We left nothing behind in that pristine area, except perhaps some flattened grass that would soon restore itself. A good lesson in "If you cause a mess, you take care of it, no matter where you are."

Help all family members understand that picking up and cleaning up after themselves will be the single most useful job they can do. Orderly surroundings are much more pleasant, easier to live in, and safer. It took me a while, but I finally discovered that if I put my wrenches, fishing stuff, and baseball gear away, when it came time to work or play I could do it quickly. I didn't have to hunt and rummage.

REMEMBER: There's nothing wrong with making a mess; that's often progress in the making. It's leaving it that is wrong.

"As you know, kids like to go camping. If you have ever camped the designated wilderness areas, the signs at the trailhead say: 'No Trace Camping Required,' 'If you pack it in, pack it out,' 'Leave the area cleaner than you found it.' Well, we applied that concept to our home when our two boys were growing up and to our grandchildren. We call it 'No Trace Living Required.' You can use the area, but when you leave, make sure it is cleaner than you found it. We make sure that we have a vacuum cleaner close by and you know what? They use it! It has been like a game, but it leaves no question about whose job it is to clean up."

"Buy three pretty colored clothes baskets (not too big) and some satin ribbon. Have your child help you weave the ribbon through the basket. Now you can go SHOPPING every day right at home! In one basket will go the things you find that belong to her, to be taken back to her room. One of the other two baskets will be for trash, and the last for things that belong to other people. I am in charge of the 'others' basket, and she handles trash and her basket. My daughter loves this and often does it more than once a day. You could play the same game with boys but call it 'hunting' instead!" My daughter is twelve but we still shop! We use real shopping bags from places like department stores and keep them around to toss things into."

Take Care of Your Own Clothes

Our sole responsibility to clothes is not just wearing them, as has been supposed for hundreds if not thousands of years. Caring for them—picking them up, hanging them up, folding them, and cleaning and disposing of them when necessary—is part of the picture, too. Our clothes keep us comfortable and enhance our image and looks, so who should be more concerned with their maintenance, preservation, and accessibility than us?

In the cleaning assembly I mentioned earlier, I picked up a clothes hanger, held it up, and yelled, "What is this?" A chorus came back to me, "It hangs up clothes." "Wow," I said, "let's watch it." I held it high in the air and we all watched it. Finally I turned toward them and said in an accusing tone, "It isn't working!"

Now the kids were a little confused and murmurs went through the crowd. "You told me it hung up clothes and it isn't working." They didn't know what to say until finally one kid yelled back, "You have to hang the clothes on it!" A big sigh of agreement swept the group. "Oh, it doesn't work by itself—*you* have to hang the clothes on it," I said. Then we had a little session on why and how to hang up clothes instead of throwing them on the floor.

Don't Litter *Indoors*, Either!

Too much of home cleaning is almost nonstop litter pickup—it's the biggest housecleaning timewaster. It also causes a lot of fights and frustration. When family members can't find something, everyone else has to take the blame as the seekers whine and stomp through the house trying to locate the articles they should have put away in the first place. Litter and clutter cause more arguments than anything except finances and are responsible for many household accidents. Taking a little time to raise awareness or change a habit can mean a lifetime of not having to pick up or hang up behind a careless clutterer.

> "Everyone wastes time searching for things that were thrown down instead of being put away properly. Teach by words and by modeling that when things are put away in their designated space it frees your mind for more important and creative things."

> "When I feel like my home is out of control, rather than ME do all the work (which I think many moms do), we collect all of the toys, stray clothing, shoes, papers, books, etc., and put them all in the foyer into piles for each person. Then each person takes those items to their room."

"We always pretend that our car has been our 'bus,' and you can never leave your trash, backpack, or musical instrument on the bus! After every trip (far or near), we carry all our belongings inside and take trash to the trashcan, immediately. The car stays clean and uncluttered this way."

"My children have to have their backpacks packed and ready by the front door before bedtime. All papers are supposed to be signed the night before. Clothes are laid out the night before."

"When my children were young I printed up a 'get ready for school' chart that had simple words and pictures to tell them what to do to get ready. My daughter especially loved the independence of doing this when she was in kindergarten."

"As parents, we often jump to the rescue when our child has spilled something or made any number of other messes, and we clean it up for them. When we take ownership of their mess, what we're really telling them is that we are responsible for cleaning up after them. We need to train them to be responsible for themselves. While we can provide the necessary equipment, they need to be the ones to do the job, even if it takes longer!"

Ways to Prevent Stains and Messes

Here are some simple ways of preventing making a mess in the first place:

- Don't carry dripping things across a floor or carpet.
- Wipe your feet when coming in from outside; take off wet or muddy shoes/boots as soon as you come in.
- Prevent splatters: don't use too small a pot or turn heat too high.
- Use the exhaust fan when cooking, especially when frying.

- Use a drop cloth or put down old newspapers before you start something messy.
- Be careful where you spray hairspray.
- Be careful how you dispose of chewing gum.
- Don't put beverage glasses on wood furniture without a coaster—it will leave an ugly (and hard if not impossible to remove) white ring.

Mess-Prevention Mantra

If you open it, close it.
If you take it out, put it back.
If you turn it on, turn it off.
If you move it, put it back.
If you unlock it, lock it.
If you use it up, refill or replace it.
If you break it, fix it.
If you can't fix it, find someone who can.
If you borrow it, return it.
If you make a mess, clean it up.
If you're done with it, put it back.
If you don't know where it goes—ASK!

"More is caught than taught. How can we expect our sons to put their dirty socks right into the hamper the if Mum leaves her socks on the floor to be picked up later? How can we expect the children to clean the toilets if Dad won't even replace the toilet roll? Cleaning up after yourself isn't a special God-given gift or talent with which only the lucky few are blessed. It's a good habit (even a virtue) we can all acquire!"

Chapter 7
Deciding and Dividing

So here we are at the big crossroads—deciding who and what and when and where.

This can be a chance to work together with the family toward a common goal. What you learn about compromise and cooperation here will carry over into other areas of your relationships. Sit down together with your mate and the other household members and decide what the cleaning priorities are and who can help out with what.

> "Our son is fourteen years old and has contributed to the household since he was a toddler. Here's how we did it: Years ago we had a family meeting and listed what everyone in the family does to contribute to the household. We listed everything we could think of and then we asked our son how he thought he could contribute to the household. We never used the word 'chore' nor did we ever use the words 'help us.' In other

words, we weren't asking him to do chores or to help us out; rather, we asked him to participate in the family by taking responsibility for contributing to the household."

"Letting kids have ownership of the problem, rather than telling them what to do, has been successful at our house. We met as a family and listed chores that are necessary to keep our home running smoothly. (Note that I did not say 'keep our home clean' as we all have different definitions of THAT!) The pets must be fed daily or they'll . . . gulp! . . . die, laundry must be washed and put up or we'll . . . be naked! . . . dishes must be washed so we can eat, etc. The next phase of ownership is the KIDS create a job wheel or whatever and decide a fair way to group the chores on the wheel."

What Is Fair?

One of the first big problems we often encounter in the conversion process is that question that keeps cropping up, what is "fair"?

Everyone big and little will throw the concept of fairness at you, and some of the logic will be so good you will be lost for an answer. I guess this is a good place as any to start teaching us all that life is not fair. Little or nothing is fair in life or for that matter in cleaning. No matter how well you decide and divide and delegate and all the rest, nothing will come out perfectly even.

In the housework arena, if you're worrying about each household member doing his or her exact share, forget it. The attitude you want to encourage is that we don't split work and expect everyone to do his or her share—we all work together to get it done. If one finishes first, he helps the others so they can get it all done faster and do something else together. It doesn't matter who did it last time; all that counts is that we end up with and enjoy a clean, neat setting. So just jump in and do it. *Don't keep score.*

"The children are not the only ones who have chores in our home. I think it's important for them to see Mom, Dad, and baby sister doing their fair share of chores."

"I have three children, and their names (as well as mine!) are on the chart with a list of chores that need to be done. They seem to be more willing to pitch in when they see Mom's name on the chart, too."

"Kids being kids, my children always wanted to make sure that each child had the same number of jobs. I had to get them to understand that some jobs were bigger than others so that they didn't have to have the same number per child."

Age and Ability

One of the biggest reasons for failure to get everyone to pitch in and help carry the communal load is simply a lack of faith in and knowledge of what tasks everyone can do. By the age of ten there are few cleaning jobs girls or boys can't do as well as you. By the age of twelve both of my daughters enjoyed volunteering to work as maids in the Sun Valley Resort. We'd have big checkouts at times when our cleaning crew was short. So not only myself and my wife would go to work to fill in, but as you usually do when you own your own business, many of the kids, too. My son was cleaning phone booths at a time when most of his friends had not yet started working, I was running an eighty-acre farm at sixteen, and even now a grandson at sixteen is managing a fast-food store, doing impressively what I (a seasoned businessman) couldn't manage to do. One night while my wife and I were visiting with a Cambodian family in the Boston area, a tiny two-year-old picked up a cloth and came over to the glass coffee table and polished out the fingerprints. I was amazed that she recognized the prints and had the power in those tiny hands to do it. And she kept at her cleaning campaign in the room for the next thirty minutes.

Kids can do real cleaning long before they are adults, and sometimes they can even do it better than adults.

Kids can use ten-speed bikes and computers, and often while Mother is hustling around cleaning up the house the kids are all huddled around Nintendos, which require thirty times the skill that cleaning does. Sure they can do it!

"Jobs need to be geared to age and abilities. A two- or three-year-old finds great pleasure in helping empty wastebaskets for several minutes but would be frustrated by a two-hour job."

"I use the height method for chores; when they can comfortably reach it, it's time to learn how to do it, clean it, whatever. By the time a kid can reach the kitchen sink, it's time to learn to wash the dishes, etc."

"I underestimated what my children could do and was really surprised the first time I had them vacuum. They did a great job and were so proud of themselves."

"Give them things to do that you USED to say they were TOO YOUNG to help with, and always have a list of things they might do next so they are always trying to attain that next level."

"My daughter is in eighth grade and homeschooled. For an elective this semester, she picked home economics . . . specifically domestic cleaning and engineering! She read *Is There Life After Housework?*, *Clutter's Last Stand*, and *No Time to Clean!* Instead of writing book reports (to clutter the file cabinet), she wrote a four-week schedule for cleaning our home and put it in practice. The cleaning tasks are shared with her brother and myself."

Divvying Up

Despite what I said earlier (stop worrying about "your share"), I know some of you still are going to ask: what is a good, or the right, way to divide up the chores between yourself, your mate, and the kids? There are no infallible rules here, but the following is usually a good approach:

- Start by having everyone make a list of what needs to be done regularly around the house. Then compare everyone's lists—there may be some real surprises here!
- Pull from the above a list of chores everyone agrees are essential, plus some you would all like to see done whenever possible. Set the priorities and compromise a little. Decide where neatness really counts (such as perhaps the living room and kitchen) and where you can be more relaxed (the closets and the garage?). How clean a house do you really want and need to have? Never forget that you live in a house, not for it.
- Divide the necessary chores among your family. When dividing up the chores from there, bear in mind the following:

  - How much time each person has available, and how much time and effort each task takes
  - The skills and abilities of each family member, age, personality, allergies
  - Degree of difficulty of different tasks (hard and unpleasant chores could count for more)

You might consider setting some time when everyone can pitch in and get it all done together. There is a reason pro cleaners often clean as a team! (See Chapter 11, pages 163–65.)

"Have a list of the estimated time it takes to complete each chore. It will motivate them and help them to know what to expect when they 'sign on' for a job."

Let Them Do What They Like?

Do give children, especially, some choices of things to do. If they are given the chance to help decide their responsibilities, they are more likely to carry them through to completion. Give them the pick of the litter (or at least a choice of two things whenever possible), and let them turn their hand to whatever turns them on. If they hate toilets, trade or clean them yourself, until you can persuade them otherwise. Let them get comfortable with cleaning and gain a little confidence first.

But do persuade them! They cannot grow up or leave home doing nothing but what they like to do. Sometime (hopefully before they face the responsibilities of their first big job or married life) they need to learn to like what they have to do. We've all run into things that we put off, dread, and wouldn't do if there were any way out. But we do them, often under duress, and guess what? These often end up being the most interesting and beneficial of all. Doing one thing only that you happen to like and are good at is okay for a while but will eventually be a drawback.

Make sure kids get to try everything. Someone once said to me, "As a child I was assigned to clean the wash basin. That's all I did. I was an expert wash basin cleaner and when I got married that's all I knew: how to clean wash basins." Let children use every tool and run every machine, run the whole gauntlet of home care and cleaning, inside and out, expose them to all areas and types of cleaning. When kids see the big picture, they get a big view (and a big capacity to clean)!

"It seems the more choices I give my kids, the less resistance I get. If they complain about a job when it comes time to do it, I remind them that they picked it out. If they argue over any particular one, I assign that one to each of them on a rotating basis."

"In all honesty, there are tasks kids just don't like to do and never will like to do. I have one child who loves to vacuum and another who doesn't mind doing toilets a bit. I have another who would rather work outside. Just as we all have our own special genius within, we probably have our preferences as to what we want to do in the way of housework. I suggest letting them do what they like and are good at. As long as they are contributing to the greater good, and putting in their hours, let's not demand they do certain things. Why force-feed peas when they can only stomach carrots? Feed the peas to somebody else! All of the vegetables will eventually get eaten."

"I list the things that need to be done and allow my children to choose their primary responsibilities. They still need to learn how the other tasks are done, but they're allowed to pick, trade, and negotiate between themselves. Giving them a choice seems to empower them and give them a sense of ownership of what they're doing."

"About twice a year, we review our son's responsibilities and revise if need be. We revise based on his maturity level and what over time proves to be the kind of activities that give him satisfaction (although not all of his contributions to the family are necessarily things he likes to do!). If he hates a responsibility he has taken on, then we discuss switching with one of us to something he might like better. If it turns out he wasn't physically or mentally ready for a responsibility (meaning that maybe he consistently isn't doing a good job at it), then we diplomatically take it off his list. This way, he doesn't feel like a failure and we don't get aggravated."

Forget the Old Work Divisions

Don't let home assignments get set in cement. Mom doesn't own the laundry room, nor Dad the garage, nor the kids the dishes. Dads can bake and make beds, Junior can do laundry and arrange flowers, Mom can wash the car, and Sis can trim the bushes. Variety is the spice of life and of cleaning, too.

I find myself suffering from the old sex division of chores around the house. Men didn't cook much when and where I grew up, and I always hated cooking—what a waste of time, to my mind, to do all that work and have it disappear in ten or fifteen minutes. So I never cooked anything. At the age of sixty-eight I finally tried making a hamburger and ruined it as a result. I also don't fold clothes—I just stuff them in the drawer. And I don't match socks—two dark or light together is good enough for me, for the drawer or to wear. Keeping these habits through my life has come back to haunt me here and there—I could have used a broader home-based education. But I was raised in a rural area, where the house was Mom's and Sister's and the outside, the barns and pastures, were Dad's and Brother's. Lots of that stuck, from childhood. In our more urban society today we need a better spread of skills and acceptances.

Systems, Systems, Systems

You do want to record the results of all this, so that everyone knows what he or she is responsible for. Some of the methods people have come up with for recording and dividing up chores are impressive, but they can take a lot of work to administer. Over the years I've seen unbelievably creative systems for managing kids' cleaning—charts and cards and tallies of all kinds. Some of these management and incentive systems are more complicated than cleaning up an entire Holiday Inn after a prom night.

Overall plans and assignments do need to be written down—in large letters if necessary—and posted where possible. But remember, too much detail and too many cards, charts, graphs, and checklists will defeat your whole purpose here. I love lists—I live for lists—but if there are too many, even I will lose or ignore them. Few people read today, and even fewer read the fine print of anything.

We can use cards and charts and the like, but we also have to watch that it all doesn't get so complex and technical that the system becomes harder to manage than the job itself. When that happens, eventually, sooner or later, the assigner (you) or the assignees (them) will cave in, and the project will wash. And since it is faster to just do it yourself, you will, and let them stay out of the way occupied with a video game. Only the government can keep overly complicated systems going.

A system is worth it if it works, though, and that is an evaluation you will have to make for yourself. There are two important points to remember here. First, systems need to be sustainable, capable of a long, continual life. We have a tendency to use stopgaps, go for instant results, not weighing how long our new little plan or deal is going to work. Second, if you set up a highly structured system, you must be disciplined enough keep it going!

Just a Few of the Many Ways to Divide and Assign Chores

• • • • • • • •

- ☐ List tasks on the family calendar.
- ☐ Create a job board.
- ☐ Draw a diagram of house or yard, color-coded according to chores of different family members.
- ☐ Post a chore chart on the refrigerator.
- ☐ Make a simple chore wheel.
- ☐ Put a card with the chore for day on counter.
- ☐ Use pictures or stickers for kids too young to read.
- ☐ Pick chores from pieces of paper put inside a hat or a bag.
- ☐ Draw straws.
- ☐ Put each job on a piece of paper and put it inside a balloon. Family members each pop a balloon, and that job is their job.
- ☐ Bake assignments into cupcakes, muffins, or cookies. Write them on slips of paper and put inside square of foil.
- ☐ Put all of the household chores (daily, weekly, seasonal) on separate cards, shuffle and deal them out equally. People can trade ones they don't like with other family members.
- ☐ Include some free passes among chore slips.
- ☐ Draw picture of chore on a card, write the family member's name on it, and have a smiley face for other side when the job is done.
- ☐ Create a spreadsheet or list on the computer.
- ☐ Assign household zones or jurisdictions.
- ☐ Make a contract.

"My daughter started helping at a very young age, but as she grew older the fun of folding washcloths and setting the table diminished. That is when our contract came into being. I sat down with her and explained that since she lived in our house, keeping it clean was partly her responsibility. We determined which chores she should be responsible for, listed them, and both signed the contract. The contract was amended as she grew older. At the same time we also negotiated a payment structure for additional work. She received a small allowance, but as she moved toward the preteen years she was happy to do more to earn more. The additional work was on the honor system and each week she would submit her itemized list of the extra chores she completed and collect her pay. This approach worked very well for both of us. My daughter is now a beautiful young woman who is an executive in the corporate world. I believe that the contract contributed, to a small degree, in her success. From those early years she learned many valuable lessons, such as negotiation skills, work ethics, and the benefits of doing more."

What Has Worked for My Readers

"What worked in our house? I created a sign-up sheet and wrote down all the things that need to be taken care of inside and outside of the house. I asked the kids to sign up for what they'd like to do rather than telling them what to do. We all do our jobs at the same time for a limited amount of time. I include a variety of things on the list that the kids might enjoy doing, such as spraying the plants or freshening up the flowers and watering the flowers. On sunny days the kids often prefer the outside chores. I've had great success with this method, and it eventually teaches them all the things required in each room to clean and tidy the space."

"I hang pictures of what their chore for the day is on the refrigerator so I don't even have to tell them what they have to do. The pictures are taken with a digital camera and printed out on regular computer paper. You can take a picture of your child doing the chore or just the chore itself (the broom lying on the kitchen floor could represent 'sweep the kitchen')."

"We used a variety of chore charts over the years, but our kids' favorite was made with poster board and wallpaper samples. Next to each child's name were two pockets: one 'To Do' and one 'Finished' or 'Done.' The night before, I placed small cards naming various chores in each child's 'To Do' pocket. In the morning they ran to see what they had to do that day. It gave them a great feeling of accomplishment to move a card from one pocket to the other—especially to see all cards on the 'Finished' side of the chart at the end of the day."

"Make a file box of jobs for each child. Have them help you cut out pictures from magazines and paste them on bright cards."

"I used a job jar. I put chores on slips of paper and everyone would draw a task. Because of age differences, I would qualify certain jobs. For example, I would write, 'If you are over eleven, mop the kitchen floor. If not, return slip and draw again.' I always included a fun task such as walk the dog, make yourself a cup of cocoa, etc. This plan worked much better than constantly telling the kids to do their chores."

"We use room stewardships. Each child is assigned a room that they have stewardship over for the entire week. On Saturday the child has to deep clean their assigned room. When they're done they have to check it off with Mom or Dad. Then every night that week after dinner, everyone must check their room stewardships and clean up as needed. They learn to feel 'ownership' of the assigned rooms and what stewardship really means. They learn that a little work each night makes cleaning a room on Saturday really easy. But my favorite part is they learn to clean up as they go. For example, if there are kids in the family room with toys, the person assigned the family room stewardship will often say 'Be sure to clean that up when you're done.' It makes a parent smile."

"You have to change your plan every so often. If you establish a job system and think it is going to last you the rest of your life, forget it. You have to shake things up and get kids motivated again. It's a bummer, but the good news is there are lots of options out there."

Let Them Know What's Needed

One big reason people often don't help around the house is because they really don't know what needs to be done. So make a list of the most urgent to-dos, and post it—it'll go a long way toward removing this stumbling block.

One year, at home and at the office, I posted a "stand around" list of things people might do to help out if they found themselves with some time on their hands. I think I can credit it with getting rid of some worthless potential sons-in-law, who figured, after reading the list, that if this was expected around this house, they were in the wrong place. Finally one young man (whom one of my daughters *did* want to marry) challenged me on one of the items listed there, which was "Put a new roof on the farm shop." He was ambitious and willing, but as he pointed out, this was a little on the heavy construction side.

But "stand around" lists can work! And you have nothing to lose; the list is just a standing invitation for family members or others to lend a hand. The failure of a stand-around list will usually be from our side, when we fail to maintain a full, fun list. So keep the projects coming and posted.

"When extra things come up that need doing, I write them on the small white board above our chore chart. I find that when kids (and husbands) have a concrete list of things that need to be done, they are very willing to do them. This has been a great help to me!"

"There are many good ways to organize maintenance responsibilities, but I believe the real secret is not in the plan but in the attitude which is established."

Some Household Jobs for Helpers

For the Little Ones

☐ Set table

☐ Wash, dry, and/or put away dishes

☐ Load and/or unload dishwasher

☐ Sweep

☐ Dust

☐ Remove cobwebs

☐ Spot clean (clean off fingerprints and smudges)

☐ Match socks

For the In-Betweeners

☐ Straighten up

☐ Mop floors

☐ Wash and dry laundry

☐ Fold laundry and put away

☐ Clean microwave

☐ Bring in mail or paper

☐ Open/close blinds or curtains

☐ Water plants

☐ Organize books, videos, CDs, DVDs

☐ Vacuum and declutter car interior

☐ Read stories to each other

- ☐ Help shop for/put away groceries
- ☐ Baking (and cleaning up afterward)
- ☐ List groceries the family has run out of
- ☐ Help think of cleaning preventives
- ☐ Pet care (feed, brush, walk, clean pet cages or houses, clean out litter box)
- ☐ Holiday preparations and undoing of same
- ☐ Yard work: raking, mowing the lawn, cleaning the yard (which often has twigs, toys, tools, and litter to pick up)
- ☐ Sweep patios, sidewalks, decks
- ☐ Help plant, weed, harvest garden

The Teens

- ☐ Babysit
- ☐ Cook (Kids often like to cook and can make simple meals, like sandwiches for school lunches. Cooking is often one of the things that is skipped or compromised when a parent is overburdened. Of course, keep the little ones away from the stove or knives.)
- ☐ Help ill or elderly family members
- ☐ Shop; carry in groceries and put them away
- ☐ Pay bills
- ☐ Make a budget for something (such as a trip)
- ☐ Make family scrapbooks/photo albums
- ☐ Take out the trash
- ☐ Put in/take out screens/storm windows
- ☐ Paint
- ☐ Small repairs
- ☐ Transporting
- ☐ Wash house siding
- ☐ Clean gutters
- ☐ Split/bring in wood
- ☐ Wash car
- ☐ Deliver things and do other errands

"My oldest daughter liked math and actually enjoyed balancing the checkbook."

"My overall goal is for my children (boys and girls) to know how to do all the jobs (cooking and toilets included) in our home before they leave so that when they are in an apartment on their own or starting their own household they will be competent to take care of themselves and their own families."

"Children should also be taught to love the outdoor chores. Help them to gain an appreciation of the growing of fruits and veggies. Show them the results of their work as you prepare the harvest in your meals and let them help you in this process. Pick flowers you grow and put a vase of them in their rooms and around your home and remark how beautiful they are and how they add to the beauty of your home. Let them help you with BIG projects such as painting the home or remodeling, no matter how young they are. Have them hold screws, paint low spots that you can go over later if necessary, and pound in nails that will not be in the finish work. This will help them feel confidence in doing that kind of work in their own homes later."

A Checklist for the Children

Children will do what is expected of them. They often do their jobs more reliably than adults if they know the what, why, where, when, and how of them.

Make up your own little attractive checklist (maybe even illustrated with cartoons) like the following for your children that can be hung up in some conspicuous spot.

I help clean our house!

1. I make my own bed.
2. I hang up my own clothes and put them away.
3. I put dirty clothes in the hamper.
4. I pick up my toys when I'm done with them for the day.
5. I scrape my plate after I eat and take it to the sink/dishwasher.
6. I take my own things out of the car when we go somewhere.
7. I put trash in the garbage right away, and I put empty cans and bottles in the recycle bin.
8. I dust.
9. I sweep/dust mop the floor.
10. I help vacuum.
11. I help fold clothes and do the laundry.
12. I help keep my pets clean.

Chapter 8
Tools and Supplies

Ironically, we often worry the most about the simplest parts of a subject. The topic of tools and equipment for cleaning is one good example of this.

I've made thousands of appearances on television and radio, and I've been interviewed by hundreds of newspaper reporters. Guess what the biggest question about cleaning usually is—the gear, equipment, and chemicals you should use. New helpers, too, often have lots of questions about this.

So as not only a pro but as someone who owns cleaning supply stores, allow me to dispel all of this wondering and give you the lowdown on the following questions:

1. What you need
2. How to use it
3. Where to get it
4. Where to keep it

"Give a kid a clean room and they have it for less than an hour; give a kid the proper tools and teach him how to use them, and you have a clean room for life."

The first thing to do is get it out of everyone's head that some magic tool or cleaner is going to work like you see on television, or at home shows and county fairs. Don't think you're missing something if you skip the aisles in the stores that have hundreds of different cleaners, including some of the same things in five or six different colors, flavors, sizes, and strengths. As for tools, in the past twenty years alone I've seen at least thirty different "magic mop" inventions that everyone had to get, try, and then shuffle to the back of the closet and forget.

The pros often have to clean huge places such as offices, hotels, and hospitals quickly and efficiently. Yet notice there are only a few basic tools and cleaners on their cleaning carts and in their janitor closets. The surfaces in homes and other buildings today (hard and soft flooring, paints, laminates, and so on) are better than ever, and they are easier to clean than the surfaces of the old days. The cleaners today are better than ever, too, and in this day of deep-pocket liability, safer than ever. So this tool thing is not going to be complicated.

The second step is to forget all the old wives' tales and "home remedies" for cleaning, using foodstuffs, toothpaste, club soda, vinegar, and all the rest. Never try to invent your own cleaning solutions—some chemical combinations can badly harm or even kill you. Forget too, about harsh cleaners such as bleach, ammonia, and powdered cleansers—you don't need them, and they can damage household surfaces as well as possibly you. *One of your first concerns in getting help is to keep the help safe and healthy,* so go through all of your old cleaning liquids, powders, and potions, and dispose of anything that isn't labeled. Get rid of anything nonessential whose label includes warnings like "danger" or "flammable" and move anything you must keep to child-safe storage.

The third thing to remember is that the name of the game here is convenience.

Most people can and will clean and care for things if all they have to do is grab the tools and go. If they have to dig through several closets and cabinets—and even then maybe never find what they need, or carry a bunch of awkward stuff all the way from here to there—they won't do it. If it is inconvenient to do a cleaning job, even I, America's #1 Cleaner, might be slow to do it. If we can clean or service something quickly, we will, but if there is any degree of difficulty in the where, when, and how, kiss cleaning goodbye, even when it comes to adults. Being able to get your equipment in hand, get right to the job, and put everything away quickly is a real key here. This means you want "multiples"—instead of one cleaning station or cleaning supply storage area, have several. Have a cleaning station under every sink, or in every room that is cleaned often, instead of in one place in the house. Remember we aren't looking at cleaning as a full day or big family effort on Saturday morning. We have ten or fifteen minutes to clean here and there these days, not to mention a short-fuse attention span—especially for cleaning.

The day of the soggy cardboard box under the sink for cleaning supplies is past. You can purchase inexpensive plastic cleaning caddies almost anywhere, and they will last indefinitely. Cad- dies are designed to be por-  table, so you can take whatever you need for a job along with you. They keep things organized and stored neatly, and bottles and other tools won't be falling over. Instead of the House of the Seven Gables, you can have the House of Seven Caddies, if necessary. You want one in the garage, too, because your second home (the one on wheels) is parked in there.

While smaller caddies are available, most standard cad- dies are fine for kids. More important is the size of what's *in* the caddy—see pages 97–98. The Don Aslett Little Joey Caddy was designed with children in mind. If you have young children, caddies can be stored in cabinets with childproof latches.

> "Make a basket with kid-friendly cleaning materials that belong to the child; paint their name on it, or put on some stickers of things they like. Dress it up a bit. Then, when you go to clean, they can follow along with their own tools, and clean things at their level (I like to have them do the baseboards, dust chair legs, stuff like that)."

If you would like, or need, a larger and more complete portable cleaning tool holder, check out the new Klean-GuRoo cleaning cart. This friendly little unit is the home version of the maid or janitor cart you see in motels and commercial buildings. It takes no more room to park than a vacuum, and it can travel with you anywhere in the house. I have one on every floor of my homes, and they leave no excuse for family, friends, relatives, or guests for not cleaning up after themselves.

Take the "multiples" approach with things like brooms and vacuums, too. Why lug one vacuum all over the house—up and down stairs, from one end of the place to the other, bumping into walls and furnishings, maybe even falling with it in the process? Second (and third or even fourth) vacuums can make sense, and the lesser amount of wear and tear on each will make them last a long time. You might even designate a machine for each of your home cleaners if you can afford it.

> "What I have done is purchase lots of cleaning supplies. I have five good feather dusters, five types of vacuum cleaner (different sizes and types for different jobs), a carpet sweeper, and a bunch of microfiber cleaning cloths. Having to share the tools and supplies never really worked. Having enough for all of us to work together has worked beautifully. The amount that we get done and the amount of time that it has saved us has been well worth the expense."

The Junior Cleaning Kit

Must we find and furnish scaled-down tools for our child cleaners? Not necessarily—a child can use many cleaning tools every bit as well as an adult. The simplicity of cleaning tools—brooms, vacuums, dust cloths, and spray bottles—is wonderful when you think about it. Sponges, cloths, dusters, spray bottles, and so on that are a bit smaller are a help for younger children. Buckets can just be filled a little less full, squeegees can be ten instead of sixteen inches, and most sponges and cleaning cloths do not need to be adapted for youngsters. One of the greatest decluttering tools ever invented, the clothes hanger, works well in all hands (as long as there is a rod that kids can reach).

"Why do you think the pediatricians tell us to keep our cleaning supplies behind locked doors? Because kids love to spray things! The one thing my six children will help with is the windows and fingerprints on door handles and trim. They love to spray glass cleaner. It's not always perfect, but it's one less job I have to do!"

"When my son was only three, I would give him a little bucket of soapy water, and he would go ahead of me, finding scuff marks and spots on the floor, and scrubbing them. I would follow him with the mop. He had a blast, and it certainly saved my back!

"My kids love having their own spray bottles, too. My daughter loved to spray and polish the stove front in our former house. She loved how shiny it would look! And they each have their own small lambs' wool duster. I painted the wooden handles with acrylic paint so they could tell them apart. I have a larger one and we all love to dust together. They love using real cleaner too. We only use non-toxic products."

"The young ones are given their own spray bottles, sponges, laundry baskets, etc., with his/her name. At the bottom of the basket for the children is a personal note from Mom in paint pen that says 'I knew you could do it,' or for a two-year-old a big smiley face. They get possessive about these things and proud of them, too. Ours just love to be surprised with those Don Aslett potty erasers (way cool with the preteen boys) when all has been well done for a time. Little ones love to get the lambs' wool duster and 'tickle' the furniture."

"My older kids love your idea to spray a lot of cleaner and then wait while the cleaner does the work. That is the only time they are praised for sitting down on the job and working smarter not harder."

Something we often forget is that a great deal of cleaning is done with *no tools at all*! Picking things up and putting them away, straightening and organizing things, requires only a willing brain and two hands and feet.

It is even more important in child cleaning than usual to buy good, sturdy equipment, in bright and attractive colors whenever possible. Experience over the years has taught me that if cleaning gear is clean and good-looking, it is more likely to be used. You could even consider personalized cleaning tools, with the names or monograms of the owners and users.

Families have reported that when the purchase of a new vacuum is made as much of an occasion as the acquisition of a new pool or bike, the kids line up to get to use it. Kids love a vacuum with a headlight!

You could even make each child his or her own little cleaning kit, with a dust cloth, spray bottle of all-purpose cleaner, and some cleaning cloths, for example.

The Family Cleaning Closet

If you do have a central cleaning closet or wall space in the utility room or kitchen for cleaning tools, work toward the end goal of having nothing touching the floor. There are all kinds of creative racks and tool-handle holders for the wall in home improvement stores. Chose one that fits your décor or personality, and wall mount as much as you can of the equipment, dustpans and all. Shelves of all kinds are good, too. Wire baskets keep things like sponges and small tools handy and allow them to dry quickly.

Taking the time to do this will return to you great dividends in getting help around the house:

1. It organizes the tools, keeps them ready, and offers an inviting place to put them back.
2. It keeps the closet clean and odor free.
3. It tells anyone who opens the closet that cleaning is important, a top priority around this house.

> " It might be good for parents to store all cleaning supplies and tools to be used by children in one place in the home. Explain to children they are welcome to use anything in the closet. And demonstrate all items. (For safety, dangerous items like drain cleaner might be best stored somewhere else.)"

Cleaning Solutions Made Simple

Four simple solutions should lead your arsenal of cleaning resources and always be within reach:

1. **All-purpose cleaner, or APC.** We pros call this a neutral cleaner, which means it is neither acid nor alkaline, just in the middle of the pH scale. It will do about 90 percent of the

cleaning needed in the average home safely and well. This will be your general or all-purpose cleaner, just as the name suggests.

2. **Disinfectant cleaner.** The type I recommend is referred to by professionals as a "quat." It contains a germ killer plus a detergent. This is what hospitals use to mop floors and clean bathrooms and the like. It cleans things and sanitizes them, which means it disinfects them to a degree (it doesn't sterilize them). Most odors and infections originate from bacteria, and this solution will kill bacteria and discourage its growth. In most cases, you want to spray it on a surface, leave it on for five or ten minutes, and then wipe or rinse it off. Use disinfectant cleaner for cleaning bathrooms, doorknobs, and other "germy" places, but not on kitchen tables or counters. Limit the use of disinfectant cleaner to older children.

3. **Glass cleaner usually contains alcohol and/or ammonia,** and its quick evaporation makes it great for cleaning glass or reflective metal. In many situations (such as on appliance fronts) it can be used almost like an APC. It doesn't streak as much or leave residue, so it creates a shiny surface easily.

4. **Heavy-duty cleaner** (such as Soilmaster or SuperOrange) is a stronger, more alkaline cleaner for tough jobs and grease removal. Limit the use of this to adults and older children or teens.

5. **Water.** Yes, plain water. Although water won't do many types of cleaning by itself, combined with the new microfiber cloths, it can do an amazing amount of cleaning. It is perfect for smaller children to use, since it is safe for them and most of what they might be cleaning.

You can buy the first four cleaners above in concentrate form at a janitorial-supply store. Buy a gallon or quart of concentrated cleaner, and dilute it in down into spray bottles per directions.

I would put all four of these solutions in clearly marked spray bottles. For children, smaller spray bottles are often available in the cleaning section of supermarkets or stores. Use professional spray bottles—they are available in two sizes, quart and twenty-two ounces. Get see-through bottles, and everyone will be able to see the color of the solutions inside and quickly learn to identify solutions with their duties:

APC is green.
Disinfectant cleaner is pink or red.
Glass cleaner is blue.
Water is clear.

All of these bottles, filled three quarters full, fit perfectly into a caddy along with the other items needed for the majority of regular house care and household emergencies such as spills.

Other Key Tools for Home Cleaning

Invest in some terry cleaning cloths. Remember, one of our big objectives here is to make people want to clean, so the uninspiring word "rag" should never be used around your house again. What you want to say and use is cleaning cloths, so don't use old T-shirts, used bras, old curtains, or other "rags." You can make your own cleaning cloths from hemmed eighteen by eighteen-inch squares of sturdy terrycloth or buy them from the Cleaning Center.

Microfiber cloths are a real advance in cleaning and are now my favorite kind of cleaning cloth. Microfiber will absorb ten times its weight in liquids, and whatever it picks up it will release instantly under a running faucet. This is a super fast and efficient tool, and it feels good in the hand. Twelve by twelve inches is a good size. One or two of these need to be in every caddy and anywhere else in the house they might be needed. They're washable and reusable.

> "I made my daughter 'dusting mittens' out of felt squares to help with the dusting. I'm not a seamstress, but dusting mittens are easy. Trace your child's hand (mitten style) onto a piece of felt in their favorite color, add a little extra room to make it easy to get on and off, and add a seam allowance (such as half an inch). Cut two for each hand. Sew on the seam allowance line. Your child can now slip on the dusting mitten and help you dust. They enjoy helping when they have their own equipment. I did this many years ago, long before the Pledge dusting mitts were thought of."

You've seen and used **nylon-backed scrub sponges** for years. They have a nylon mesh pad on one side and a sponge on the other. I always keep two types around. The ones with a white nylon pad can used in the bathroom and anywhere you need scrubbing action with no risk of scratching. White scrub sponges are best for kids.

Sponges with the more aggressive green pad are used only when tough scrubbing action is needed on surfaces that can take it. These can be used (instead of your fingernail) to remove stuck-on dirt. If you use them wet, as you should, they will glide over the surface safely and only snag the little lump or deposit of dirt or hardened catsup.

Get professional-size scrub sponges from a janitorial-supply store and keep them in the caddy too.

A **grout brush** is like a miniature scrub brush with a long handle or an improved version of the old toothbrush many of us have used to clean tight spots. The stiff nylon bristles on the small, narrow head are just what you need for cleaning cracks, edges, grout lines, and anyplace you can't reach to scrub with a scrub sponge. These are small and fit kids' hands nicely.

A **handled scrub brush** or "utility brush" has firm, springy, long-lasting nylon bristles that really reach into corners, crevices, and uneven surfaces to remove the dirt. The long handle keeps your hands out of soil and cleaning solutions.

The new nylon and plastic molded **brooms** are far better than the old straw or corn brooms. These can be a wee bit smaller and still get the job done, especially since most of us don't have the huge hard floors of long ago. The majority of home floors are carpeted now. For this same reason, you don't need a huge **dustpan.** All you need is a small easy-to-handle pan that can be kept in several places. Have one hung or tucked away anywhere you sweep frequently. There are brooms now (and some mops, too) with telescoping adjustable handles, which are well adapted for kids and which delight them, too. A hanging broom is far better than a leaning one—don't warp the bristles by leaving brooms sit on their heads.

Don't forget that neglected broom—the push broom. Get one with an eighteen-inch head with angle braces, and keep it in the garage. You don't want a head larger than twenty-four inches. Push brooms are great for large areas and can sweep everything from fallen maple leaves to sawdust or a light skiff of snow off garage floors, patios, sidewalks, and driveways. Kids really love these. Remember, any dirt, dust, or debris that you get rid of outside and around the house won't be tracked indoors.

"Our twelve-year-old daughter, who is our official sweeper, has come to expect fancy new brooms whenever she gets an award at school. She likes her zebra-striped one best. For Christmas this year we gave her a hot-pink striped one

and she beamed at us saying 'Awesome! I thought you
might have forgotten.'"

Lambs' wool dusters look like cotton candy on a stick.
You might call these an improved version of the feather duster,
and they come with either short or long handles. The pros
have used these for years, and now you see them on television
and all over.

Buy a genuine wool one, not a cheap synthetic, and it will
grab the dust and hold it like a magnet. These can reach, and
be used on, almost everything in the house, and they pick up
what they don't knock to the floor for the vacuum. Even dead
bugs and cobwebs will stick to them and can be vacuumed off.
When the duster gets dirty, gently hand wash and rinse it out.
They will last a lifetime. Best of all, they are fast, fun, and easy
to use, and anyone over three can dust with one.

If your home has lots of delicate breakables or chan-
deliers, it would be good to also have a professional feather
duster. A pro duster (such as those made by Texas Feathers) is
one made from real ostrich feathers, which hold dust instead
of just knocking it loose. A light flick with these will remove
dust and any other light debris. There are even long-handled
feather dusters for high dusting.

A **Scrubbee-Doo or hand floor scrubber** is *the* indis-
pensable tool for hard-surface floors. Most people are still
doing the old hands-and-knees routine, but this is what they
should be using. I've gotten rid of most of the old mops that
I used to swear by and now at home use mainly one of these.
A hand floor scrubber is a long handle with a flat plastic Velcro-
covered swivel head at the end. Attach a four-by-eight pad of
microfiber to the head, and you are ready to mop anything.
You don't even need a mop bucket. Just sweep the floor first,
and then spray it quickly and lightly with APC. Leave the solution on there for a minute or two, and then mop the floor with
the pad. The pad will loosen, pick up, and hold an amazing
amount of soil, and when it is saturated with dirt it can be

quickly rinsed out by hand in the sink. Floor care is so fast and efficient with this that it is actually fun.

There is almost no getting-ready time required for the hand floor scrubber. There is a thirty-second setup and thirty-second cleanup, and it stores anywhere. The handle is also adjustable, so you can easily make it the perfect height for whoever is using it. It is light, safe, and inexpensive, and will last for years. The handle, head, and mop head only cost about $25, which means you can have more than one mop around the place.

A variety of other heads are available for a hand floor scrubber, such as a dust mop, wax applicator, and nylon scrub pads. Dust mops (the dust mop head of a hand floor scrubber, or a regular pro dust mop) will clean large areas of hard flooring more quickly and easily than any broom.

Every bathroom should have its own **bowl cleaner and bowl caddy.** Deep cleaning the toilet is a twice a year or so job that adults (or children over sixteen) can and should do to keep toilets clear of hard water deposits that not only look ugly but will also eventually make a toilet hard to flush. Bowl cleaning equipment should not be kept anywhere the little ones can access, and it should never be used by anyone who doesn't know how to respect possibly harmful materials.

> "Children, like adults, are more willing to work if they have the right tool for the job. It makes it easier to accomplish the task and it is more fun. So tell them that when the floor is picked up they can use the cool vacuum."

There are thousands of models of **vacuum cleaners** on the market. I did national tours as a publicity spokesman for one of the major vacuum companies, and they alone had been through 247 models. You have choices of every imaginable size, type, and style of machine, plus all kinds of better-than-ever bags for them. *You vacuum as you need to, not by schedule.* If there isn't much traffic or floor fallout in a room, it can go weeks or even months without vacuuming. If you have a tribe constantly running over the carpet, plus several pets, it might need daily attention. The bottom line here is to have an easy-to-use vacuum right where it is needed. I'd get a small one for kid country and a nice professional-quality upright (easy for even kids to use, from about the age of seven up) for the rest of the house. For high and detail vacuuming, a small, easily carryable canister is good. Large battery powered units for the most part are too heavy, and they often have poor suction.

Have a vacuum in the garage, too, preferably a wet/dry or shop vac, which can be rushed into the house when the tub or toilet runs over or a pipe breaks.

When buying vacuums, buy quality and buy once—those cheap vacuums that seem to do miracles in demonstrations are only a miracle if they work very long. Reconditioned vacuums are often every bit as good as new ones, so you can often save some money here.

> One of the most important considerations here is size! You want a vacuum that fits the user and the situation.

For the little ones, there are small lightweight canisters with reach attachments. It isn't out of the question to put a small personal vacuum in every child's room—a feeling of ownership generally encourages use. Dragging a big vacuum out and then all around the house has always been a pain. I like the little Top Vac ($29) for quick pickups of small stuff like crumbs or dead flies on windowsills. A vacuum like this will fit in a drawer. Adult or teens should do all bag or filter changing.

"If a kid is old enough to push a toy vacuum that makes fake noises, then they can certainly push the real one (safety first!) that's louder and actually WORKS. 'Look Honey, this one is so much more fun!' The littler they are, the closer to the rug they are and can see the crumbs and dirt best. Besides, let's face it, it's mostly their ground-up crackers on the carpet anyway."

"Sometimes, the oldest two will actually start fighting about who's going to vacuum—now that's an argument I LIKE to hear."

Have a **window squeegee set** within reach. No matter how dirty windows get, normally no harm is done—they don't rust, rot, or wear out. However, dirty windows can do some damage to the image and spirit of "clean" around the place. "I don't do windows" is a remark we often hear, but window cleaning is easy and actually fun, if done the professional way. Plus, it costs very little to do. You can buy a pro window cleaning kit (lifetime set of equipment) for around $50, which includes a magnificent pro squeegee, a wand to apply the cleaning solution, a bucket, a scraper, and best of all, an extension handle that eliminates most ladder work. This means that even a ten-year-old can do a good job of window cleaning without hurting him or herself. And better yet, a dollar's worth of dish detergent such as Joy will clean all of your windows for the rest of your life. The learning process is quick (as described in *Is There Life After Housework?*). You can even buy holsters for squeegees, and there are little golden squeegee pins you can reward little cleaners with for a job well done. Best of all, this can end up a part-time job and real moneymaker for the teen cleaner. I know a high school senior who made $2,000 the month he graduated cleaning windows!

A good squeegee can be a super contributor to family peace and income. It's a nice gift to give a kid when he heads off to college—he might be able not only to pay his way through school but send checks home to help support you!

These are the basics that can and will take care of most general cleaning—let's not get lost in the scores of specialized products that might be used for certain things only. There are a few additional things you might want to add to your cleaning kit: an all-purpose spotter such as Perky Spotter, an odor neutralizer such as X-O, bacteria/enzyme digester for pet messes on absorbent materials like carpet or upholstery, and a pet rake for easy pickup of pet hair.

Avoid the "purely for play" child cleaning gear. It might have a little value at the very youngest ages for following Mom, Dad or an older brother or sister around and playing with it while grownups use the real thing. But most toy vacuums, mops, and brooms don't really work, or work well, and they soon break, disappointing kids and adults alike. Most of the "big people" cleaning stuff outlined here can be used by little people.

Cleaning Safety for Children

Too many people are injured in or around cleaning projects, and there is no need for this. Climbing, slipping, falling, and mixing or using the wrong chemicals can all be eliminated by using the simple basic cleaners described earlier, plus extension handles as needed for high dusting, high windows, and the like.

Here are some guidelines now to make sure we head off any chances of injury in our new world of child cleaning.

Rule #1: Remember the Curiosity Factor

Kids are energetic and inquisitive and will find, reach, and try out anything, anywhere. They're all too likely to be wondering things like "Will the vacuum suck up water?" or "How much Windex does it take to kill an ant?" So bear this in mind when you do any assigning or instructing in cleaning.

This is the day of attractive packaging, and just about everything, including cleaning products of all kinds, has nice, bright labels that can lure kids to try or taste. Kids these days can figure out safety lids better than we can.

Get serious about safe storage. Keep bleach, bowl cleaners, and all garden and pest control chemicals in a high, hidden, or locked place. Bear in mind that big, heavy buckets or containers of even less dangerous things, falling or pulled down from a shelf, can injure or kill a child.

> "At four years old, our son moved his bed away from the wall in his quest to conquer the dust bunnies that lurked beneath. He located the dust buster and attempted to remove the filter. I explained to him the dire consequences of that action and advised him to keep it intact. A few minutes later, a loud wailing could be heard from his bedroom. An explosion of dirt completely covered his bed, as he had relieved the dust buster of its filter and turned it on in an attempt to satisfy his ever-constant curiosity. After taking a few calming breaths, I presented him with the central vac, and he set to work to clean up the shrapnel. Seconds later, another loud wail was heard. He had vacuumed up the dust-buster filter!"

Rule #2: You Do the Mixing

Kids can police an area by themselves, but clean alongside your children when they're using cleaning solutions. You measure and mix the solutions for them so you can be sure what goes in and how much, the temperature of the water, and so on. Most household cleaning doesn't require strong chemicals, just a little waiting for the solution to do its work and some occasional "elbow grease."

Keep the child cleaning kit confined to mild water-based cleaners, such as all-purpose cleaner. You can let older kids use a spray bottle of disinfectant cleaner if you're with them, but you or one of the teenagers should do anything that involves

the use of bowl cleaner and any other dangerous products—
always!

Rule #3: Don't Let Kids Climb to Clean

Kids love ladders, ledges, and rooftops, but make "feet on the floor" the rule for young children. Don't ever let a young child stand on anything to clean, period. If they want to clean higher, they can use long-handled tools.

Older children can do some modest climbing to help clean, but don't let them choose the climbing vehicle—they're all too likely to pick a hassock with wheels, a shaky chair, or a stool with a narrow base, any of which can easily slip out from under them. Use only the special safety-designed, non-slip stepstools or miniladders.

Rule #4: Electricity Alert

Teach children to stay well away from anything electrical with wet hands or water in any form. Make sure they understand why, so it doesn't make them curious. You can let them use extension handles on dusters indoors, but put an eight-foot limit on any extension handles outside the house to avoid any run-ins with electrical wires. (Nobody can see the dirt on anything higher, anyway.)

Rule #5: Adults Only

Many modern tools, from mowers and trimmers to electric knives and scissors, are not the old hand-operated variety. Most are power tools that you just plug in and push a button or turn a key to start. They're so simple that a two-year-old can figure them out. Any power tools used for cleaning should be stored out of sight, locked up with the key removed.

Let children vacuum, but they should not change bags, belts, or anything where they might get their hands in the mechanics. Don't let very young children work with beater-bar vacuums or power wands, and make sure children of any age know to keep their fingers well away from the working parts. A canister vacuum is safer for a small child than an upright.

Rule #6: Glass Safety

All of that plunging through windows that we see in movies and on television can lead children to believe that glass is harmless. But falling through windows and other glass surfaces and getting cut while trying to pick up broken glass account for many injuries of children and teenagers too. Make glass a no-no for your youngest cleaners.

Rule #7: Bucket Safety

Don't leave buckets full of water or cleaning solutions out around very young children. A small child can drown in a few inches of water. Keep toddlers away from automatic washers and dryers, too.

Rule #8: Trash Savvy

Taking out the garbage is a good chore for older children, but putting garbage in a wheeled plastic can or other secure and/or closed container is a better way of handling this chore. Garbage in plastic bags alone can contain dangerous things like broken glass, sharp bones, and protruding metal things. Plus, kids tend to like to drag the bag, often tearing it and spilling garbage everywhere. Don't let kids snoop in garbage. Any trash-carrying to the road needs to be supervised.

Rule #9: They're Not Toys

Never let kids use cleaning gear to play with, such as using spray bottles for squirt guns or riding on vacuums. Don't give them any vacuum crevice tools or edge cleaner attachments to use unless they have a notch in them for safety and you are supervising. Kids can and will hold attachments like this up to their faces while the vacuum is running, and serious injury can result.

Safe Cleaning Jobs
Any Child Can Do

Sweep
Mop
Make beds
Dust
Remove cobwebs
Put dirty clothes in the hamper
Sort and fold their own clean clothes/put them away
Help sort and match socks; fold washcloths and towels
Sort books, videotapes, DVDs, toys, shoes; put them in order
　　(sorting helps young children build their cognitive skills)
Sweep or hose patio, sidewalk

"I have discovered that there is sometimes an underlying reason why some children balk at cleaning. It's not always an aversion to the chore itself. Foul-smelling chemicals that burn their sensitive noses or skin can be a major turnoff, and they may not even be aware of what is causing them to hate cleaning. Getting them their own kid-friendly cleaning supplies that smell pleasant (my kids like citrus) and rubber gloves (small medical exam gloves work very well) make the chores more pleasant. Also since I discovered your products (that actually work!), they feel like they are truly accomplishing something rather than just moving dirt around."

Chapter 9
Some General Advice for the "General" (Mom)

Having a simple, conveniently located collection of the right tools for the job doesn't guarantee they'll always be used. Unfortunately, none of these time and/or work-savers we've discussed will operate without human power.

Someone has to be the leader here to see that things happen. Someone has to see that there are cleanliness standards, has to help divide the chores, and has to make sure they are carried out. That means that you—yes, you—are the benevolent general in this war against clutter and dirt. And your family (hopefully) will be the "troops" that fall into line.

As you enlist the troops into your family's own housekeeping philosophy, here are some ideas that may help—ideas our family and other families have used.

Use Standards Rather Than Schedules

Before trying to draw up a comprehensive cleaning schedule, set up and use another type of tool—standards. Standards are a commitment to maintaining a level of cleanliness that allow you, me, and them to work out the details. Well-established standards can all but eliminate the need for detailed specifications or schedules. A detail assignment of "Clean the corners once a week" means you also have to schedule what day—say Tuesday. If a mouse dies in the corner or an apple core gets dropped there on Wednesday, you will have an unacceptable situation for the next six days if you are simply following the rule. A simple standard, on the other hand, would be "Don't let the corners get grungy." The corners can then be cleaned to need, not schedule. You might not need to clean them for two months, but there may be times they'll need attention twice in one week.

A standard is kind of like a covenant we make with our house, a codification of expectation. It simply sets a quality level and allows you the freedom to decide when and how to reach it. Thus standards eliminate much scheduling and assigning. Standards let people find their own answers to "when" and make their own adaptations in the "how." We all like this. I hate people outlining my schedule, and I think most people, young or old, feel the same.

Standards simplify things. What is the difference between standards and rules? That is the beauty of it. Other people enforce rules; standards, you enforce yourself.

Especially when time is short, it makes more sense to clean to a standard ("The kitchen floor shall look and feel clean") than to a schedule ("The kitchen floor must be mopped every other day"). The standard "Walls shall be free of handprints and smudges" makes more sense than "Wash the walls once a month." Standards establish how clean you want something rather than how often it should be cleaned.

Using standards gives you a destination rather than a deadline. Standards don't pin you to the clock or calendar. Instead, they pin you to the task and allow its timing to be at your discretion.

"Clean Home" Policies

In addition to standards for the actual cleaning of different parts of the house, you might want to consider some more general standards or policies for your home to help keep it presentable and minimize cleaning. After you draw these up, you might want to post them for everyone to see, read, and follow. These expectations apply not just to family members but to guests, visitors, and grown children back home again.

Home-Care Standards

Here are some sample ideas you might want to adapt and enact for your own house:

1. Cleanup is done NOW, not later. Housework is done before homework.
2. Clean first, play later.
3. This is a home, not a hotel—we serve ourselves.
4. Each of us is responsible for our own guests.
5. If something (paper towels, toilet paper, etc.) runs out while you are using it, replace it.
6. Dishes not in use are put away.
7. Beds are made when you aren't in them (as soon as you get up).
8. Mail and newspapers are read (or trashed) the same day they arrive.
9. All trash is trashed as soon as it is created.
10. Clothes are either on your body, on a hanger, in a hamper, or in a drawer.

11. Counters and sinks shall be free of clutter, crumbs, spills, and dirty dishes.
12. Furniture is in its place and used for what it's designed for.
13. Pictures and posters shall be on a bulletin board, framed, hung neatly, or in a scrapbook/album.
14. All cleaning gear will be left ready to go.
15. Food shall be stored where it belongs and tossed when outdated.
16. The house will be left in an orderly condition before we retire at night.
17. Cars are never brought back empty of gas.

When Is It Best to Clean? Regularly!

This is a good place to address the often-asked question, "When is the best time to clean?" The answer is easy—regularly! Letting things go, build up, or get messy is shooting yourself in the foot, even if you make it a family affair or turn it into a cleaning party. The old saying "Life by the inch is a cinch, by the mile is a trial" is very applicable to cleaning. It is the same as letting the dishes and counter go until later, and then doing them all at once a day later. This may sound efficient, but it doubles the time it takes to clean and makes us dread it. Hanging clothes up while they're in hand beats picking ten articles off the floor and chair backs a day or two later. (Plus, it saves hunting, apparel abuse, and arguments.)

This is the same principle we pros use on spills, spots, and stains—"A spot is *on* and a stain is *in*," we say, and the difference is in the timing. If you get a spot or spill on something, especially fabric or carpet, for the most part it is removable, thanks to soil retardant in the material. But leave it there until later, and you'll have a stain and spend a half hour and all kinds of chemicals on it, with doubtful results.

Cleaning a bit every morning or every day is faster, better, safer, less boring and tiring, and leaves Saturday morning clear. Wiping the sink right after you use it, disposing of trash right away, taking dishes right back to the kitchen, and putting dirty clothes in the hamper right after you take them off is so logical. *Later is a loser in cleaning.* The instant availability of resources (tools and cleaners) in caddies gives no reason to wait. Why enslave yourself to "later"? And best of all, consistent little daily cleaning will help cultivate a positive attitude toward cleaning.

Keep ahead and early so housework is a minor, not a major task.

> **"I am a firm believer in keeping up on housework every day. It only takes my kids five to ten minutes a day to do their daily jobs, maybe half an hour on the weekend–so that when Friday and Saturday come, we can play without guilt!!"**

> "It is so much better to tackle the small job like wiping the bathroom sink in a minute each morning than to spend thirty minutes scrubbing a week's worth of splashes. Prevention is often the key to avoiding feeling overwhelmed."

> "Often our kids' rooms would be a horrendous mess through the week, but they knew they had to clean up on Saturday before they could do anything else. After a while, they learned that if they didn't let the room get out of control messy, far less of their valuable Saturday was spent cleaning. It's always best if they can learn these things through their own observation. The parent's job is to set it up so that can happen."

Some Important Things to Remember

Watch Your Own Attitude

Being a good example is extra-important when it comes to the actual doing of the chores. Kids pick up quickly on any kind of negativity.

> "I think the most important piece of advice I can give is to let children see that you are enjoying what you are doing. If you hate cleaning and grumble every time you have to do it, what are they going to think about it?"

Start YOUNG!

Most parents who have actually done it feel that two or even younger is not too soon to get started, and by the age of five or six children can have regular chores. This principle is so important I have devoted a whole section of this book to it—see pages 173–80.

Be Nice!

Even the kindergarteners I polled on this said, "Say please." Just about every human being responds better to suggestion and motivation than to threats and orders. Most of us know better than to approach grownups that way—don't let your standards down just because you're dealing with youngsters. Questions and discussions are better than commands and demands.

> "My husband and I believe that parenting is about guiding children, not punishing and demeaning them when they don't do as we say. We involve our son and ask him what he thinks and how he wants to contribute rather than telling him what to do and what he should think. I think this is why our son willingly (for the

most part) contributes to the household. And why he's a happy, responsible person."

Start Small

Don't give kids too much responsibility right off the bat. Make sure chores fit their physical strength and skills, and don't give a child more than he can handle. We all like, and want, to succeed!

For younger children, you can break jobs into parts or stages. Don't ask them to "clean their room"—start with just one specific part of the job, or corner.

"Break overwhelming jobs into small bits."

Keep Cleaning Sessions Short

Kids bore easily, so keep it short, ten or fifteen minutes at a time. Try to avoid big, long stretches or marathons of cleaning, such as the big Saturday morning siege, where we do all the cleaning in one big block of time every week. We adults get tired of this and come to dread it, and kids, with their limited attention span, get tired of it even sooner. Better to break the cleaning up into little daily install- ments. For instance, do one of the seven things  each day instead of all seven on Saturday. You'll enjoy the work more. Besides, it'll be done better (because you aren't tired of cleaning), and you won't resent the cleaning because it's cheating you of your favorite Saturday-morning activity.

A book about housework was published many years ago with the title *Never Done*. That is exactly how we don't want housework to be viewed, as work that never ends. Cleaning in smaller installments, even time fragments, is much more appealing because you can "be done" any minute.

"Lawn mowing, weeding, and other chores in and out of doors are best shared with breaks for cool drinks and fun. A very short-term goal helps to entice the reluctant helper."

"When my children were growing up we practiced the ten-minute pickup. After dinner was done each night, I set a timer for ten minutes. Every person in the house had jobs, and during this time, we did as many of them as we could get done to beat the timer. One person might be picking up toys, someone scrubbing the toilet, someone else dusting. There were plenty of jobs to do, but ten minutes is a LOT of time if used wisely. When the timer went off, we stopped and then enjoyed time together."

"Whenever things start getting a little cluttered, I tell my kids 'It's time to clean ten!' They rush around, each putting away ten things. It can be anything they want, as long as they know where it belongs. It usually takes about two minutes, and with four kids, that's forty things back in their right places. When things are really bad, I tell them 'We need to clean ten and then clean ten again!' "

"With a timer, kids know there is a time limit, and they know exactly when they will be able to stop. It is actually fun to see how much you can get done in five minutes. And it is amazing how many of those jobs you put off 'because they will take too long' can be done in under five minutes."

Make Sure Your Helpers Know What You Expect.

This step is covered in detail in Chapter 11. We often assume that helpers of any age know exactly what we want, or how something needs to be done.

Don't just spring it on them. When it's time to clean, or you want something done, try to give your helpers some advance warning, even if it's just a half hour. This gives them a sense of control, the time to psyche themselves up, and a chance to finish up whatever else they might be doing. Outlining what you want done the day or week before is even better.

Remove Distractions If Necessary

This may mean draining the swimming pool, hiding the remote, shutting down the computer, and taking the car keys.

"Make sure television and video games and such are off in the entire house before you/they start."

Don't Forget: They're Not There to Help *You*

Remember always, in your speech and actions, to avoid creating the impression that the other family members are there to help you. The appearance and comfort of a home is of concern to everyone, it is "ours"—every member of the household has ownership in it all, even those garbage cans!

Remember also that kids are different. This means the same approach, tactics, and incentives will not

work on all, because children, like we adults, are all different in personality and temperament.

"Finding out what is important to a child is one of the most important things. We are all so different and our priorities are different—but I would begin by saying win your children's heart, and they will gladly serve where needed."

"Remember some people do things at different times of the day. I am a night owl—I get more accomplished in the evening or after everyone has gone to bed. Let your children choose the time to do their part, within reason. Let them choose a system that works for them. Not all people do the same task in the same way—respect that in your child also, this helps them to learn about themselves and others who may do things differently than they do."

Be consistent—stick to your guns.

Few revolutions happen overnight—they take time to accomplish. More about this on pages 213–16.

Strategies for Success

Beyond the basic principles described above, successful housework-sharing parents have devised an amazing variety of ways to help assure that young people become enthusiastic members of the family team. Creativity often blooms when the stakes are high, and our hard-won knowledge of child and adult psychology—what turns people on—can be a real assist here. One or more of these ideas is bound to work for you, if you don't think of something better yet!

Make It Fun

"Housework, children, fun? Do these words even belong in the same sentence?"—Home and household writer Rachel Webb

I've spent my life selling the underrated and often disliked job of cleaning to the world, and I've been successful at it (some would say wildly so). My secret has been simple: I've made it fun. Make work seem like play, and it will be!

Cleaning doesn't have to be a dreaded "better do" duty. It can be incorporated into games, races, skits, and music. It's better than a coffee break for visiting and thinking and letting your imagination run wild. If you would like to see some of the creative ways my company and I found to make cleaning entertaining and even inspiring, check out the book called *How to Upgrade and Motivate Your Cleaning Crews.*

> "My children are at an age when they actually fight over who gets to clean the toilet because it's FUN! I don't know how long this will last before one of them leads a revolt, but I'm going to milk it for all it's worth!"

> "Folding laundry and doing dishes is a group effort for our family. In time the children developed games to play during the dishes to pass the time—'Guess the movie,' 'Guess the person I have in mind,' or just plain singing together. It has

become a joy to sit in the living room and hear the fun going on in the kitchen! Of course there are those nights like every other home where small disagreements disturb the fun, but they are few."

Cleaning to Music

Anything that might spice up cleaning activities is generally well worth the effort to implement. Music is inexpensive or free, and its ability to strengthen resolve and energize us mentally and physically is undisputed. Work like cleaning that doesn't require full concentration or focus can be enhanced by music, so make use of it whenever you can. For safety's sake, use a boom box or CD player near the work area rather than headphones. Peppy music like marches is what you want, not slow, languorous tunes or sad melodies. Better yet is composing your own personalized family songs to old familiar or favorite tunes. Little ditties like these will be hummed for a lifetime if taught in youth. This will enhance both the kids' enjoyment of music and the work itself, especially if you let children pick the piece of music (out of a group preselected by you).

"Turn on their favorite music, sing, dance, whatever you can do to make it fun and a special time that you spend together. These times will become memories that will last a lifetime."

"One of my favorite ways of having everyone help out with the housework when the kids were young was to play an upbeat song such as: 'Dirty Laundry Boogie' by Tom Knight. The boys would scrub away the dirt as they sang along with and danced to the music! It seemed like the chores took no time at all when we played lively music while we cleaned the house together!"

"Although my girls are grown, one thing that encouraged them to help clean was music. I would put on their favorite tunes . . . put one slightly damp (clean of course) sock on one of their hands and a clean dry one on the other, and then give them a chore: Clean the table, wipe the patio door or whatever, and off they went !! Wiping . . . drying . . . and dancing!!"

Make It a Treasure Hunt
Who doesn't love a treasure hunt!

"We like to do scavenger hunts. I'll hide little construction paper shapes, treats, etc., under things that need to be picked up and put away. The kids get to keep whatever they find."

"Weeding becomes fun when you hide treats in the garden."

"We hide coins around the room in places that they will not find unless they do the job properly. (Like taped to the vacuum handle, under the bottle of window cleaner, or in the shoes that are lying on the floor.) If the job is done well, they will find all the coins that you left."

"To get my kids to wash the dishes after we ate I used to throw some change in the sink and fill it up with soap and water. When they finished the dishes they loved to find the money and keep it. It always got the job done!!"

Floors and More

"I like to make cleaning a game. Put a basketball hoop over the clothes hamper in their room. That's an easy one."

"One sure-fire way to get the floor scrubbed really well is to let them use their feet! A small bucket, lots of rags, and some big thirsty towels to dry up with is all it takes. They love it and beg to do it."

"When the kitchen floor needed a good scrubbing, I would let the kids 'ice skate.' I would put their Daddy's work socks on them (those socks were always gross, anyway), put some water with floor cleaner on the floor, and let them 'skate.' They had a great time. The only rule was they had to use their toes and get in the corners. When they were finished, I took the socks off and threw them in the washer—they often came much cleaner for being 'pretreated.' I would then put the exhausted kids down for a nap, and do a quick mopping to pick up any leftover solution/dirt. Once we had friends over and I let all four kids skate. The friends' Dad called me and said his daughter had excitely told him, 'Brianna's mom let us mop the kitchen floor!' He wanted to know what I was doing over here!"

"When older kids are squabbling give each a bottle of glass cleaner and a microfiber towel. Put one child on one either side of the glass. They can squirt at each other and get their mad out as they clean the windows."

"I was a preschool teacher for seventeen years, and I learned from the start that it has to be fun for kids to get involved. I have dumped plastic washable toys into a water table with lots of warm very sudsy water and old toothbrushes. Shaving cream is a good cleaning agent, but children need to be old enough to play with it without it ending up in eyes or the mouth. Make sure too that what you're cleaning is shaving-cream safe."

Bring out the Drama in Cleaning

This can be something as simple as using puppets to play "pick up toys." You can also try giving your child a spray bottle of water or all-purpose cleaner and asking if he wants to play "magician" to get the spots off the kitchen floor.

"You and your child can pretend you are the innkeepers of a bed and breakfast. Let him or her dress up in some kind of uniform and grab a fuzzy duster. Then strip the bed, load up the bath towels, and show how to do some laundry. Then remake the bed together. I gave my daughter an old key with a plastic tag, which she decorated with the name of our B&B. She pretended to use it to open the door to her room at cleaning time."

"I raised two daughters, and one had a favorite television show that involved the army. One of the things she learned watching it was about keeping things neat and inspection routines. For her, our housecleaning became a game of getting ready for weekly inspections. Mother played the supervising lieutenant who did the inspections, and daughter did the cleaning and putting away of things. This game worked long enough for it to become a habit."

"We had a 'Clean Fairy' that came to the house and checked on the kids' rooms. You never knew when she might come. If the room was picked up then the Clean Fairy would leave a treat of some sort. She always left a note telling what a good job they had done and why they got that treat or a note telling why they

did not get anything. Our treats were usually pencils, papers, books—that type of stuff. If one room was immaculate and the other was just a bit off, the clean one might get a cool pack of pencils and the 'not quite' room would get just one pencil. The Clean Fairy used ink and paper for the notes that no one had ever seen before, not just something from around the house.

Find a Way They Can Do It Fast

Kids love fast! Provide a way for them to do whatever needs to be done faster—sweeping, spot cleaning, dishes, vacuuming, window cleaning, whatever. Reduce the time something takes and the chances of it being done improve! Let the kids think of their own ways to speed up jobs—once you approve them, they're on!

Put the Competitive Spirit to Work!

"Here is something that works with my children. COMPETITION! Every morning we have a bed-making race.

Someone will yell from somewhere in the house, 'On your mark' and everyone answers with 'Get set, GO!' and everyone drops

To help children (and adults) clean faster, check out my action-packed video, Is There Life After Housework?—ninety entertaining and educational minutes on how to clean like the pros. Kids will watch it over and over.

Send $19.95 plus $3.00 for shipping to:

Life After Housework Video
P.O. Box 700
Pocatello, ID 83204

(or call 888-748-3535.)

You can also get a copy of the book *Is There Life After Housework, 2nd Edition.*

what they're doing and runs to their room and makes their bed. It's fun, the kids enjoy it, and, best of all, the beds are made."

"With my third graders, I use complimenting strategy. I say, '_____ is doing such a great job cleaning so and so,' and the other children will want that kind of positive acknowledgment. I also say okay, I'm going to give you fifteen seconds, let's see who can get the most garbage picked up. It is hilarious to see them run around trying to be the best."

"We 'buddy' our children up, an older with a younger one. Then I divide the house into zones and assign each buddy team a zone. It becomes somewhat of a competition to see who can finish their zone quickly and well."

Make It a Race

"Make a small list of kid-friendly jobs, put a whistling teakettle on, and have a race to see how many jobs can be done before the kettle whistles."

"We play 'Count Down.' I tell the kids that the coats are going on the rack in ten, nine, eight . . . You should see them scramble! When I just tell or ask them to do something it doesn't accomplish much. But telling them that something will be done in ten, nine, etc., achieves amazing results! Sometimes I count down from five, other times from three, depending on how quickly the job can be done."

Use Some Psychology

Another thing that cuts our chances of getting any help around the house is that we often unconsciously cast cleaning as a negative. We will hear parents say (or yell threateningly), "You better behave or you will have to clean your room!" Teachers or professors say, "Okay, students, you better do well in school or you are going to end up a janitor." Thus cleaning is always a negative, a punishment, a dreaded low-class have-to. Turn that thinking around, and make cleaning a privilege!

Make It a Privilege!

"It never hurts to make it sound like a privilege to be old enough to do something–'Wow, you're finally big enough to haul out that bag of trash and bungie it down all by yourself!'"

"Start with attitude. Not 'I Have To' go to work, clean my room, do the dishes, etc., but 'I Get To' . . . remembering we are blessed to have a job to go to . . . blessed to have a room to clean . . . blessed to have a kitchen to cook and do dishes in, etc."

"I made it a reward to get to help Mother around the house. I would say things like 'If you are really good you get to help me load the dishwasher.' Or 'You have been so good today I will let you help me sort the laundry.' You have to start really young on this. As they got older they didn't think it was such fun to help Mother."

"I would have cleaned the Taj Mahal for my aunt because she never asked—she used the old Tom Sawyer approach. If she was at the ironing board when I visited her, I would watch how she carefully pressed a shirt and folded it so it wouldn't wrinkle in the drawer. If I asked to do one, she would say it was too difficult for me and I might scorch it—but here was a

pillowcase I could do, or a hanky, or a sock. In those days we
ironed everything! Soon I was doing all the 'flat stuff' under
careful supervision, then pleated skirts, and eventually I would
be allowed to press a blouse. Same with learning how to use
a feather duster—at first I was allowed to do only the legs of
chairs and tables, working my way up to shelves of knickknacks.
I worked my way up in her dishpan, too, from spoons to glasses
and fine china. She had a way of keeping my interest in what she
was doing without saying a word. My aunt cleaned as if it was
the most important and valuable thing she ever did, as if her
possessions were priceless jewels to be cared for and her lessons
were a privilege to attend. And they were!"

Appoint a Chairperson

"Everyone likes to feel in charge. You can give kids
that feeling of control by putting them in charge of
one area in the home and then giving them a title:
Chairperson of Pets, Chief Sweeper-Upper, Assistant
Gourmet Chef, Toy Coordinator, Co-engineer for
Maintenance, Archivist (the one put in charge of the
family scrapbook and photo album)."

Try Reverse Psychology

"I have found out that the best way to get my two-year-old and
four-year-old daughters to help me clean the house is to pretend
like I don't want them to help. The less I seem to want help, the
more they want to help!"

Establish a Routine

"Children love routine, and if you have a household routine
in place, the children will come to expect certain things to

be done at certain times. And believe me, if you forget, the child is certain to remind you."

"One of the biggest keys to success has been a routine (Monday lights washday, Tuesday darks washday and groceries, Wednesday pay bills, etc.). It takes out the argument and the delay of deciding what we're going to do today, as long as we're willing to follow through with it. And the chores get done without all piling up. Plus the kids know there's a definite time and a definite end."

"My kids clean for half an hour at the same time each day. In the past, when I haven't had a schedule and surprised them with 'It's time to clean,' it was a great struggle."

Teach by Degrees

"My favorite is to be 'progressive' in my teaching. When they are young, start with a part of a chore (emptying a certain part of the dishwasher), and keep adding parts as they grow older till they accomplish and are regularly responsible for the entire chore. Then, when that is mastered, have them be in charge of that chore or area for a period of time (for example dishes or laundry). You become much more accomplished at a task when it's your 'baby' for a time."

Trade Children!

"My answer to kids doing cleaning is to trade kid(s) with another family. For some reason your kids work better for the other person and their kids work better for you. This is more for major cleans than just picking up their own room. It is an adventure to go to another house to work and much more interesting."

"Trade children for the afternoon of the clean up with the neighbors, or your relatives living nearby. When I was a child I always liked doing things for other people better than for my own family. No sibling squabbling over who made the mess in the first place."

Change the Vocabulary

"One of the tricks I came up with to get the kids to help with housework was to use the word 'literacy' when describing learning to do a task. It is a way of describing the task at hand as a kind of power they would be gaining rather than a burden that as soon it was learned would be dumped on them. One of our first goals was 'laundry literacy.' It was learned and practiced in the summer. It became a way of being proactive about taking care of stain situations that could potentially ruin the article of clothing involved, enabling them to prevent a bigger problem from occurring. Around our house this approach worked."

Encourage the Creative Touch

"I encourage my children to finish their job by doing something to make the clean room or area pretty. This is the fun part of homemaking. The child who sets the table is encouraged to decorate it or make homemade place cards, which we all notice and thank her for. The child who sweeps the front walk way can move a potted plant to the porch or put a decorative item there. This gives the child an extra sense of accomplishment."

"In our home everyone is responsible for his or her space. Including children, in decorating their space, it helps them to 'own' their area."

Write It Down

"I have used a list system for eleven years, and it has worked better than any other idea. The lists vary with age and ability, and as the children become older the lists have added responsibilities. I put every responsibility they have at home for the day on the list including homework, music practice, etc. The kids know that they must do the things on their list as soon as they get home from school, or first thing Saturday morning, before they do other things. While my children complain about the lists once in a while they know that they are a fact of life in our house. Overall there is not a fraction of the complaining that there is if I ask them to do a job without putting it on the list. For example, if I ask my thirteen-year-old son to vacuum the stairs he will gripe and complain and we will both end up in a bad mood. If it is written on his list, however, he just does it."

"A schedule is just a tool, not a slave driver! I do find, however, that we get a lot more done when we have something written on paper than we do when it isn't. So it's just a handy tool to keep us focused and reminded of what needs to be done."

Vary the Program!

"Not all ideas will work all the time, so the key is to have a variety of responses so that you have options. You may go through several with one child, or find one that works consistently. When the excitement goes out of one thing you have to change to something else to keep them interested. The key is to remain cheerful and firm, and you will form a child who cheerfully and willingly helps out."

Chapter 10
What's in It for Me?
Rewards for Young Cleaners

Maybe this chapter should be titled "Why Should I?" It may be the most important chapter of all because here we want to fill that big gap between our expectations of our helpers and their point of view, which can easily be summed up as, "What's in it for me?" That question, which crops up in every endeavor today, is the key to pulling people past intentions and commandments to some industry.

There have probably been more creative rewards invented for getting people to help clean and care for the house than we can imagine. Unfortunately, rewards are seldom thought through and followed through. Too many of them are inspirations of the moment, stopgaps, or acts of desperation. If not handled properly, rewards turn into bribery, and soon you are not able to handle the demands.

But rewards can work. Every man has his price, and this is even more true of kids. Adults grow narrow and will jump through the hoop for money. Kids learn this by the time they're teenagers, but before that they are sensitive to rewards like praise, love, travel, time spent with them, or a chance to go on a trip with or work on the job with Mom or Dad. Rewards shouldn't just be a matter of "I do this and thus I get that." Whenever possible, rewards should be bigger and more meaningful: "I do this and I will become that," or "I do this and that will happen to my life."

A Big One: Recognition

We've talked a lot about the principles of expectation and involvement. To make ours a complete, truly powerful one-two-three approach, let's add a third principle: recognition.

We all respond to recognition—timely recognition of the right kind has a power and value that goes way beyond money, things, and privileges. Especially now, in a larger-than-ever world, we can all too easily become numbers or ciphers, seeming to lack identity. Who of us wouldn't respond better to sincere praise than to a few extra pennies? (Okay, sometimes the pennies are a form of praise, or at least they reinforce it.) We all live for approval and acceptance—keeping score is often the foundation for the secondary recognition or tangible rewards, but it is the measurement itself, the score and who accomplished it that really matters.

Why else would a man or woman keep a bullseyed target from the range, or a kid cling forever to a ratty stuffed animal he won at the fair or a spelling-bee blue ribbon? We can see the cleanliness of the room someone just cleaned and that it's more pleasant to spend time in afterward. It seems as though those things should be reward enough, but they aren't. We all want recognition for what we do, and cleanliness is often such a fleeting condition that significant recognition is hard to give, and it's hard to feel a real sense of accomplishment. This is not just a kid thing—it is a human thing that probably affects adults even more than children.

For years, when we measured or rated cleaners' work in the professional cleaning industry, we always thought it was the final score or number they were waiting for, but it wasn't. The power was in the fact that somebody cared enough to look at their work, that someone recognized that they were doing something valuable. The cleaners weren't really dreading inspections, we discovered, but looking forward to having the bosses come in and see what they had done. Our scrutiny kind of gave the message that we were aware of their existence and appreciated their efforts. That was reward and praise in itself, without management's even saying anything.

Remember when you design and set up a reward system around your house that any scoring system is secondary to the real reason your helpers have for doing any task—approval and praise. Success—succeeding, excelling—is always motivating.

> "At 4-H camp, cabins are inspected after breakfast every day. Then at lunch we make an announcement as to which cabins get the clean cabin award for the day, one for a boys' cabin, one for a girls' cabin. This is mainly a verbal reinforcement, although we might let the clean cabin winners go first in the lunch line, or be the first to leave the lunch table."

> "Expectation is more than hope. It means training and follow up. And praise, praise, praise! It's not enough to assume they know you're proud. You must look them in the eye, into those little hearts, and tell them. They'll do anything for love."

> "Most people like to be praised in front of other people. A good word from Mom or Dad in front of the other parent, or visitors, will be a motivating force."

Keep Those Compliments Coming

Never give one compliment for a clean room. Give ten compliments—during and after, over and over! Clean will then become a praise they are eager to earn.

> "Don't underestimate the value of praise. Most of us can last all day on one sincere compliment. Just make sure they are genuine compliments—even young children can tell fake."

Reward in the Results Themselves

This is the ideal reward, of course, and well worth trying to make happen. Help your kids appreciate the satisfaction of a job well done when they pick up their toys or help create a litter-free lawn.

"A few hours ago, my son asked me if he could use some of my cleaning supplies to go clean the basement at someone else's home where a youth group meets weekly. He had organized a group of teens to clean and put the room in order. He explained that he likes to clean because it gives him a great sense of accomplishment and satisfaction!"

"No other rewards are necessary—the pride of having done the job well is reward enough. Children's self-esteem soars when they've done a good job and are told so, and also, as they realize that they're needed and are a valuable part of the family. Our home is filled with a wonderful spirit of love because of their willingness to do their household chores."

"Let a job well done be your child's reward. We never paid our son for helping around the house and yard. If he wanted to earn some extra money we would find something out of the ordinary for him to do. Our goal was to prepare and train him for real life as a husband, father, and homeowner."

Time with Parents

Another big motivator is the time that we and our children get to spend together. Too much of the time that technology and our helpers' cleaning efforts saves us ends up working in reverse—the time saved just allows Dad and Mom to spend more time at the office and become more distant.

Kids want your time. If all time saved in home care were clearly given back directly to kids, you'd soon have the cleanest, neatest, most clutter-free place on the planet. Too often, we reward and recognize children by giving them stuff that just breeds more disorder. Give your time, your undivided attention, to them. Just about any kid would clean for a parent's time. An hour reading or playing with a kid for every hour saved in upkeep will keep the kids focused on a real reason to respond to chores.

"When everyone is done, don't forget to praise and thank them for a job well done. Play a board game or watch a favorite video in the pleasant-to-be-in home you've worked so hard on."

Other Fun Things

My daughter Elizabeth has a great reward system for home care and cleaning. Her kids love to go to "Grandpa's farm" (my ranch), so she keeps a reward bottle where good behavior is rewarded by pennies or notes added to the jar. When the jar is full, it's time again to go and visit Grandpa. The kids thus associate clean with fun times and are encouraged in the habit of cleaning and picking up.

"One way we encourage our kids to complete their chores without nagging is with a Friday family fun night that is for everyone who has finished their chores for the week. It's always a surprise (game night, movie, ice cream out, or maybe a special outing) and it only takes one time of not being able to participate to keep it from happening again. It's worked great for us!"

"I make cleaning a prerequisite to many things. For example, if they want to go somewhere, I advise them that I won't take them until they clean up the inside of the car. If they want to have a friend over, I tell them they can't until they bring their laundry down. If they want to use the computer, I advise them that they need to dust the office first. I try to make the chore quick and simple so they can feel the immediate satisfaction and enjoy the reward they have earned."

"We use technology as our carrot. Although we have no television in the house, we do use videos and DVDs. For every minute spent cleaning our children get back minute-for-minute time with the television, computer, Gameboy, Game Cube, whatever."

"Children LOVE to procrastinate their bedtimes! So, to make a win/win situation, about half an hour before bedtime, I tell them 'Whoever wants to stay up has to clean.' If I see someone not cleaning, he/she is taken immediately to bed, so they learn that Mom is serious about this!"

"If my daughter wanted to have a party, before she could decorate and have the party, she had to tidy, dust, mop, and vacuum the entire house. Her bedroom also had to be straightened and cleaned. Motivated by the thought of a party, my daughter would efficiently spring into cleaning action. Otherwise, it was like pulling teeth to get her to clean much less make her bed. Kids have to see some tangible benefit to themselves."

Guests as Reward

Another principle that works is to encourage your kids to invite and have their friends over, always and only to a clean room. This cleverly puts the pressure for a presentable "pad" on the visitor, and the kids aren't cleaning up their mess but rather preparing for a guest. It's always better to present a job in the light of positive "get to's" rather than negative "have to's." This not only keeps rooms cleaner, it also teaches consideration and respect for others. Don't let this turn negative by taking the wrong approach: "You can ask Harry over, but clean your room first!" Far better to say something like, "Have you got things ready for Harry yet?"

"Offer some spontaneous awards for doing their chores-'Of course you can invite a friend over today, your room looks sparkling!' Or to celebrate the whole house being clean, take off on a picnic."

Prizes

Give a little prize or treat to young children at the end of each cleaning session.

Some parents have an auction on the weekend using play money paid all week for help, auctioning such things as the chance to pick out your own snack at the store, gift certificates, or deciding what movie the family watches one night. Others give their children coupons, play money, or tokens for each chore done satisfactorily. At the end of the week or month the kids can turn them in for a reward or privilege of their choice.

"Something I have done that works is giving 'Mom's Bucks' (they can be traded in for prizes or real bucks, whatever works for your family and age group). Each activity needing to be done is worth so many points or 'Mom bucks.' After the activity pay the bucks (I used old Monopoly money), and at the end of the week have the children add up their bucks to see what they want to get. It can be a video game, movie, lunch out with Mom, coloring books—the list is endless."

"I use incentive charts that you can get at teacher supply stores, and for each day that they do all their chores by a certain time, they get a sticker on the incentive chart. I keep assorted candy or books or other small prizes on hand to give them when they fill a chart with stickers. They look forward to getting their stickers each day and getting a prize for filling their charts."

"Since my oldest daughter was two we've used a 'treasure box.' She has a picture list (since she can't read) of things 'To Do.' For everything she gets done she gets a star. After six stars she gets to pick something out of the treasure box. The treasure box is filled with things she picked out at the store (this eliminates her thinking she gets a prize every time we go shopping), books, dollar store items, and occasionally candy (from her Halloween bucket, and other holidays)."

"My kids have an old PlayStation. They want a new game system. We had a discussion about responsibility. If they want an expensive new system, I told them I wanted their rooms cleaned more often, and with less prodding, and I wanted to see more willingness to help with daily chores like kitchen cleanup. They still require reminding about the rooms, but only reminding. And after-supper whining has been virtually eliminated."

- I have a drawer full of toilet erasers, toilet pencil sharpeners, toilet key chains, toilet earrings, squeegee tie pins, little squirting toilets, molds for chocolate outhouses, certificates of appreciation, videos, and books (T-shirts, too)—everything imaginable to help draw attention to the values of clean.
- Make a list, and keep it current as your kids grow, of the things they like or want most, their favorite things. This is a strong reward if you connect giving or getting these things with "clean."
- Have a kid list what they would like in exchange for a clean room.

*The best device for clearing a driveway of snow
is a kid who wants to use the car.*

Food as Reward

Whether raw carrot sticks or Snickers bars are your idea of a treat, there are times and places when nothing moves youngsters like the thought of a snack. If goodies are taken into account in a young person's total calorie intake, chosen thoughtfully, and balanced with plenty of active exercise (which cleaning can certainly provide), this time-tested incentive can work.

"When all else fails, I have been known to shamelessly bribe with ice cream. This tip works better if it's instant gratification—they see the ice cream waiting for them. (I do that with myself . . . reward myself with ice cream I cannot have until I'm done. I'm forty-seven, but it still works on me!)"

"When I was about nine, my favorite chore was shoveling snow, then coming in and my mom would have made me either hot chocolate or tomato soup and a grilled cheese sandwich. I am going to do that for my kids when they're old enough."

"About fifteen minutes before dinnertime, I would tell the kids that we would eat as soon as all the toys were picked up and put away (or whatever chore needed to be done). They would take care of something like this in very short order because they were motivated; otherwise it could take hours."

"Have a contest to see whose area is the shiniest! Have a reward pizza party at the end of the week if everyone gets all their chores done."

Money, Money, Money as Reward?

I agree with all the experts out there on child development who say that paying money for household chores can come back to bite you. The responsibilities of caring for a home are part of the package of life, and there are noncash incentives around that are better. Too many times, if money is made the reason for doing something like cleaning up after yourself, it persuades children to love money and not the value of cleanliness for helping us have a better life. Certainly there is enough suggestion around that it is money that makes the good life and is the ultimate answer to all needs.

> "Rewards every so often are good, like a movie, etc., but if you pay your kids, you will not be able to afford them one day."

> "Our kids got an allowance, but we never tied the allowance to their responsibilities around the house. We made it clear that they were getting an allowance so they could learn how to manage money and they have jobs around the house to compensate for the privilege they have of living in a nice house with nice parents (although they might not always think so)!"

> "I don't pay my children for chores; rather, I emphasize the fact that I work two jobs, and that their contributions are every bit as important as mine."

The trouble with carrot-dangling is that it ends up self-consuming—when and if you run out of carrots, everyone suffers. And we will run out of carrots as our children grow older. That having been said, sometimes the old filthy lucre does do wonders for filthy rooms!

Modeling it on some of our incentives for extra work in my company, I made up some little "Extra Jobs for Extra Money" cards. My kids all had their regular jobs that were expected of them around the house, such as dishes and bed-making. But these cards were for projects and jobs a little out of the regular realm of duties. I would fill a bunch of these out, describing an extra job we needed done on each card and putting a price on it. Then I put them a rack like the ones that hold brochures in a hotel lobby. Then, when a kid needed money or was struck by a bolt of ambition, he or she could scan them all and pick something out and do it. Then when they brought it to me with a documented date of completion, I would pay the agreed-upon price. This worked well for a while. But all good plans have to be sustained.

When plans like this fail, it isn't usually because of the kids but rather the adults, who get too busy and drop the ball. As for this one, because I was expanding my business then into many additional states, I didn't seem to have the time to keep scouting out and listing the jobs and keep the cards up. So when the kids went to the rack there were no cards to pick from, and I was off traveling somewhere. So they stopped going to the rack. Boredom and difficulty in implementing move in fast, so whatever reward system you choose, make it simple in principle and practice.

This is kind of like those "employee of the month" plaques we see on the walls of fast-food restaurants and other businesses. The purpose of these is to feature an outstanding employee each month, to give them praise and recognition. This is a good idea, but how many of these do you see current? Often they are several months behind, as whoever was in charge of this (picking the employee, taking their picture, and getting the engraving done) was on vacation or whatever and then just forgot about it, or it got lost in the shuffle. So the praising plan almost becomes a punishment, giving exactly the wrong message: Who really cares? So whatever you start, be sure to see it through.

I'm not saying to completely avoid associating cleaning with monetary rewards, but use wisdom and think out the long-range message you will be giving. Sometimes a temporary payoff may get people on the right road and into a habit they might keep after the money runs out.

I had a good thing going for quite a few years with my grandchildren. When I showed up at their house, there was always the much looked forward to (and also dreaded) "Grandpa room inspections." Being a famous pro cleaner gave me some real authority here. I would show up when expected or sometimes when I just happened to be in the area, with a handful of dollar bills. If his room was clean enough, the child in question found a dollar lying on the bed. They were little then, and they loved getting that dollar and putting it in their bank or taking it to the store. To build the excitement here, I started checking the closets, too. (Kids' closets are almost always a mess!) If the closet and other unseen areas in the room were clean, they got two dollars.

If my wife and I were staying a while, I'd tell anyone who didn't pass muster that I'd be doing one more inspection before I left. Often the reason they didn't get the dollar the first time around had been rectified. Once in a while, when even the closet was clean and the toys are not only picked up but *lined* up (and it was close to Christmas), I dropped a five-dollar bill on that bedspread!

Kids grow tired of deals, and they grow older and expect more. So as my grandchildren grew older (as we do with employees), I upped the ante. Eventually the reward grew to $5, but it was less appreciated. One day I showed up at one of my granddaughter's rooms and there were two dollar bills and a note taped to the outside of the door, saying, "Forget it, Grandpa, it isn't worth it." The room was so destroyed it would have been worth more than $20 to clean it up. That's how much finally they expected, and a great tradition fizzled out. But it did work for a while!

> Don't fail to remind kids of the time-honored custom: any money found while cleaning (short of Mom or Dad's weekly paycheck), such as change or small bills found on the floor, under cushions, or in the laundry is now the property of the industrious cleaner.

A Profit-Sharing Plan

Another possibility is an incentive that has worked well in businesses (including my own) to get people to buy in. It does use money, but only as leverage to accomplish the conversion of "the house" to "our house."

How about a profit-sharing system, where you aren't just doling out money but your helpers are earning it by their own efforts, jointly with you? In fact this plan will benefit the adults in the household as much as the children. As I mentioned in Chapter 5, the whole family should know exactly what it costs to live in and run a home and what it costs per day or month to be there.

The young people in a household may not be able to do much about mortgage payments or taxes, but everything else in the house—the cost of gas, electricity, water, trash removal, phone, cleaning, repairs and replacements, insurance, clothing, paper products, linens and cosmetics—they can and will influence. So chart all of these costs. Post the average, and make sure everyone understands that the family has so much in income to cover all of these costs. However, if we turn out lights we are not using, avoid wasting hot water and gas, and do whatever we can to prevent damage, every month the money saved goes into a rebate fund, just like company profits in a profit-sharing plan. At the end of the year everyone will get an agreed upon percentage of this or you can just split the fund equally. (Dad may keep a closer eye on this fund than on the NFL ratings.)

This fund could also be the source of long-dreamed-of special vacation, or it could help pay for college. It teaches some important principles while helping to keep things nice around the house. Everyone will be looking forward to the bills each month for a change, to see how their behavior affected them. Once there exists the possibility of a profit pool that is partly theirs, the entire family rejoices when and if someone does something that benefits it. The kids will be reminding each other and encouraging the adults to toe the line. There is something about building a savings account from good behavior, with a goal in mind, that sustains the effort. Implementing something like this might cause some raised eyebrows, but wait until you see the results!

Families that clean together glean together.

Let Someone Else's Money Make the Point

Odd, but have you ever noticed how a kid from eight to eighteen will work for someone else's money? I've hired young people of all ages who clean and work for me like desperadoes, yet their parents tell me they won't or haven't turned a lick at home. There is a wedge into the problem here, so encourage (and even set up) cleaning jobs for your kids with other people. This gives them a chance to see clear-cut results in "the real world" from cleaning—it's not just the old business of "clean your room."

> "Have a reward and a consequence program for doing chores. Decide as a group how rewards and consequences will be distributed . . . give each chore a score (some chores are harder to do than others).

Use stickers of smileys to track chores completed for younger children, and quarters for the older children. Add points up weekly for each child . . . the highest score will be the weekly winner. Example: getting to stay up an hour later . . . have a friend over . . . dinner and a movie with just Mom or Dad. Think of a big reward for your child if chores are done consistently for a month."

The possibilities of incentives and rewards are not exhausted. There are millions of parents out there with at least as many ideas for getting everyone involved in helping around the house. So never just give up on ideas or assume they are dumb.

Once you decide on your reward program, follow through with it. As you probably already know, one of the all-time most important rules for dealing with kids is this: don't disappoint them.

Chapter 11
Teaching HOW

And now, at last, the nitty-gritty of teaching kids to clean. Even if you didn't need their help right now, you'd want your bright young offspring to know how to clean quickly and well so they could care for themselves and their own families some day. In my seminars and other public appearances, I meet an amazing number of new young householders who haven't a clue about housework because they were never taught how. Their parents, unlike the parents of old, were too busy or never around to teach them, or they didn't consider it a priority.

So be sure that you *do* take the time to teach your children the right way to do all of the basic household cleaning operations—the fast, efficient, professional way. If you haven't yet read my other books and learned how yourself, see pages 158-59.

> "Many people tell me how mature and responsible my kids are, but they were not born that way. Parents have to take the time to train them, but it's well worth it in the end."

"It takes time and patience to train and sometimes retrain a child to do chores, but it's very nice to sit down after dinner and hear the dishes being done instead of doing them yourself."

Example: Still the Best Teacher

If you want a shortcut to influencing people, it's hard to beat good old example. Seeing not only makes believers, it teaches patterns. Example is still the best and most effective way to teach anything.

Let the Little Ones See You Clean

Giving good example can start very early. Many mothers of young children have asked me, "What do you do with kids when you clean?" One time-honored approach is to do most of the housework early or late while the little ones sleep. It's better, however, to have the child with you in a baby backpack or walker so the little one can watch you clean happily (fake it if you have to). This will set a pattern for both attitude and technique that the child will be eager to imitate.

"Actions speak louder than words. Trying to teach children with words is a losing battle."

"Be a role model. If you want them to keep their rooms clean and pick up after themselves, you need to be consistent in doing the same thing. No more overshooting the laundry hamper, leaving papers on the kitchen table, dishes cluttering every available surface, piles of unfolded laundry in the laundry room. Kids are like hawks—they watch to see if what you do is consistent with what you say."

The Power of a Father's Example

In my research for this book, one great truth emerged: one of the most powerful influences on whether or not kids clean is the father's example. Kids usually grow up believing cleaning is done for them by a woman (usually Mom) and most parents (and many books and articles) say to kids: "Help Mommy," reinforcing the idea that the job of cleaning belongs to Mommy. When the father cleans, not to "help Mommy" but because something needs to be cleaned, it makes all the difference.

Where the father pitches in and does cleaning, picking up after himself and not saying "your sink, your vacuum, your washer," to their mother, the kids grow up not seeing cleaning as feminine or just for others.

Example from the father is lots more effective than rules pasted on a bulletin board. He doesn't need to give stirring speeches; just the simple act of doing some housework without being asked will do much more to change the attitudes of family members.

We men don't spend much time reaching and teaching our children. By doing the cleaning we are a living lesson plan going through the house. Housework is one of the few handy opportunities we have to gain our children's respect, and show them how to be loving, thoughtful beings. Don't let it escape!

If there is no father in the home, you can still come up with a male example to offset the idea that "Mothers (women) do the cleaning." Almost everyone can find an uncle, grandfather, friend, or local hero to ask to be a "clean example" for the kids—we are just attempting here to give the message that it is okay, even macho, to work around the house. Even part-time fathers should be aware that their example in home care, even just on weekends or when the kids are at their place, is important. Cleaning together can and should be part of the package of their time with the kids. If all else fails, there are fictitious men (such as Mr. Clean) and living legends (such as me on my housework videos—see page 159) you can use.

Work with Them

Most of the kids who won't clean have never heard a positive word about it or ever been taught how to do it. We par-ents have become commanders, senders, delegators—we are much too important and overcommitted to do anything with our children. We say, "Go wash the car, "or "Go clean the yard" again and again, when "Let's wash the car," or "Let's do the yard" would be much more effective. The majority of adults have never cleaned a room with their kids. They either do it themselves or browbeat kids into it. Include yourself in the process—having Mom or Dad working with them is almost an irresistible attraction for a kid. Then motivation, instruc-tion, and habit can all be developed at the same time—plus the work really gets done! And the togetherness is great.

Kids aren't looking for a boss or an overseer for their cleaning assignments; they are looking for a coach. Busy hands always beat a moving mouth in getting a message across. You can for-mally sit a fourteen-year-old down and lecture about the value of self-esteem and discipline, or you can visit and converse while you clean together. You tell me which will have more impact.

Showing takes about a tenth of the time as telling and is much less exasperating. And when do we have better one-on-one time?

"The best way to get our kids (six, five, and two) to help clean is to work with them. We can tell them a hundred times to pick up their toys, rooms, or whatever, but if we just spend a few minutes and work with them, they love to clean up. Our daughter even made up a song when she was just three years old that said, 'Cleaning together is so much fun. Working together is so much fun.'"

"Kids are easily overwhelmed when given new tasks. They don't know where to start, how to organize the job, and what exactly they are expected to accomplish. Therefore, it is a good idea to work alongside them until they gain enough skill and confidence to do the task on their own."

"I've found that everyone doing chores at the same time is a help—rather than one watching television or playing video games while someone else is working. Even though we may not be in the same area or doing the same thing, we're still a team working together to have a pleasant and healthy living environment."

Some of the family jobs on the farm I grew up on were picking rocks and weeding beans. Both kept us in the field all day, but our parents worked alongside us, and we could talk, visit, and compete. It was then I learned that a little hustle to get the job done faster was smarter and got more praise and results. And working up a sweat made work fun!

Demonstrations for children don't have to be a sit-down class or "follow me around" instruction period. The magic words are always, "Here, let me show you how." You can simply make a brief stop in the regular flow of things and say, "Here's the way I do it—you try it!" Older children and close friends or uncles, aunts, or grandparents can be almost as influential as parents here.

"Every now and then, I start our cleaning day by showing them the right way to clean something (i.e., how to dust blinds, how to take everything off a shelf before you dust). Some days are better than others, but they are improving every time we clean."

Among the several hundred thousand people aspiring to be pro cleaners that my company and I have hired over the past fifty years, there have been many young people who were never taught to clean. How did we teach them to clean? For the most part, with OJT: on-the-job training. We put a new pledge with a good doer for a few nights. When you find a winning cleaner among your helpers, have your newest recruit, or anyone who seems to be struggling with the learning process, partner with the star. This will do a lot of educating.

"When the kids are too small for a task, I pair them with a bigger sibling. They always have fun and don't feel like they are faced with such a huge task on their own."

You can also reverse the demonstration, letting them—your mate or kids—clean something while you watch, nod, clap, cheer, or whatever. Ever notice how people turn into performers when they know someone is watching? Whenever you see good cleaning results or even just someone in action cleaning, don't forget to do some demonstrating of another kind, that of your own pleasure, and recognition and praise for the person doing it.

As you work with them, help your children learn the right way to do things, the techniques and fine points, so that the job won't have to be done over because it didn't come out as expected. That cuts out tons of negativity. "This isn't clean!" a parent said to a kid who thought she had done her best, undoing all of the preceding encouragement.

Again, the magic words are "Here, let me show you."

For learning how to clean every part of the house the quick professional way, I recommend a video I did a while ago called *Is There Life After Housework?* It includes all of the basic household cleaning how-to's demonstrated live—it is fast and funny and kids will watch it several times. If you want details on all aspects of twenty-first-century home cleaning, get yourself a copy of any of these books: *Is There Life After Housework?*, *No Time to Clean!,* or the *Cleaning Encyclopedia.*

> "Use a four-step process when introducing a new job. First you do the job, narrating as you work, while the child watches. Next do the job together. Third, have the child do the job while you watch, coach, and encourage. Fourth, the child is now ready to go it alone. If you neglect training, you open the door for battles since you both will be operating under different expectations."—Elizabeth Pantley, parenting educator

Do be sure to teach your new cleaners the right techniques and tools to use. With their strong chemicals, machines, bleaches, splashes of strong solutions, and harsh scrub pads, a careless cleaning crew and process can do more damage to a home than time and use.

Give Clear Instructions

If you want to get the results you have in mind, you must give clear and complete instructions. This is true of helpers of any kind or age, and even more so with children.

> "Remember that children are like visitors to a foreign land when they first start cleaning. They need everything explained and demonstrated. If they can read, tape a list of everything that needs to be done in each room somewhere in that room. For example, put a list inside the bathroom cupboard that tells them exactly what to do to make the bathroom clean

because their idea of 'clean' and yours may be radically different! Then walk through and actively teach your children each step of the process."

"Clearly define expectations. Be very clear what the chore means . . . does cleaning the kitchen mean sweeping and mopping, wiping the table and counter, making sure the sink is clean and clear of dishes, etc.?"

"When my children were five or six, I made chore cards for them. I took an index card and put the title of the chore at the top (Sweep Kitchen) and listed 'What you need' (broom and dustpan) and 'What you do' (1. Sweep the whole floor; 2. Make sure you move the chairs; 3. Brush the dirt into the dustpan; 4. Dump the dustpan into the garbage can; 5. Put the broom and dustpan and brush away)."

"I wrote out step-by-step instructions for specific chores, such as cleaning the bathroom or the kitchen, and laminated them. The first few times, I would do the chore with the child, explaining the process as we worked. Then I would watch as the child did it herself, and I would make corrections or offer encouragement as necessary. Finally, the child would be able to clean by herself, and I would just inspect the work when she was finished."

Allow Extra Time for Training

When you clean with children, be sure to allow extra time for training, and accept the fact that they aren't going to do things exactly as you would. Yes, you could do a better job in half the time, but you want and need to teach them how. Don't just do the job for them, out of frustration. Your persistence will pay off as cleaning becomes a habit for your kids.

"Cleaning class" may be discouraging at times, but don't give up. For a while, maybe even months or years, your children's cleaning may have to be redone, or their work might be of little actual help to you. But your child is learning. As children get older, they can help a lot more and even do major jobs themselves.

One way to speed this process is to teach your older children one skill at a time and let them perfect it. Window cleaning, for example—teach it carefully to one of your children. From then on, that is her job. She will become very good at it, and her work will actually help you. After that child perfects the job of windows, move her to another chore, such as bathroom cleaning. After a while she will become good at that, and so on. After a few years a child will be good at a number of jobs, and the rest will fall into place.

> "Take the time to show children how to do a job, and be patient waiting for the benefits. It will take time for them to learn how to do a job well, and they will probably never do it exactly as you do. It is a good test of grace on your part."

As for how much time it takes a new helper to do a task, who cares, really, as long as it gets done? Most people want to get done so they can get on to something else and will gradually set their own speed. Pushers always try to change the plod-a-longers, which usually amounts to interference. I can clean windows ten times faster than my wife or my kids, but that doesn't mean they can't or don't clean windows as well (and maybe enjoy it more!).

Don't expect all of your instructions or demonstrations to take hold the first time around. Few projects or programs work for kids or, for that matter, anyone who is just told or shown something once. Learning takes repetition, repetition, repetition.

> "Just realizing that in some respects teaching children is always a challenge and the results probably won't ever be perfect (some kids are just naturally cleaner and more responsible than others!), helped me to relax and enjoy the process of teaching rather than focusing on getting the job done exactly right."

Train One to Train the Others

A mother with seven children told me, "I train only one child to do a job—the oldest! If he can get one of the younger kids to do his job to the necessary specifications, more power to him. This means he has trained them to do it and probably will not be able to get them to do it for long without rewarding them in some way. As long as that reward is not as large as the one he is receiving for the completed job, this is a satisfactory arrangement that teaches him management skills. When the younger child does the job suitably without supervision, the job is added to his chart and I pay the reward to him instead of to the older child."

Team Cleaning

My company often cleans as a team instead of one oppressed cleaner cleaning alone. How did this come about? We had an eight-story building to clean once, and to do it eight cleaners worked eight hours every night, one on each floor. This meant the lights on every floor were on all this time as everyone was solely responsible for "his" or "her" area. Then we tried putting all eight people on one floor at a time. One person got rid of the trash, one dusted, one cleaned desks, one cleaned the bathrooms, two vacuumed, one straightened up, and one took care of spots and stains. Suddenly we were able to clean the whole building in six hours, and the lights were only on one floor at a time, which won us an official award of recognition for energy saving. Plus, there was less piddling around and no foot-dragging—the team members motivated and disciplined each other. We humans are social animals, so naturally we enjoy performing in groups more than alone in a vacuum (pardon the pun).

When more than one person cleans at once, the job takes on the spirit of a team effort. Team cleaning is faster and more fun, and it even makes cleaning a social experience. You can't really ignore the old adage that many hands make light work.

They do, especially in cleaning. Once everyone knows you're all in this together, some bright spirit will set the pace and watch everyone try to match it!

If you have a gang living at your house, you probably have a mega-mess. See if you can get the whole gang together for just one hour of group cleaning. You'll see results, not just arguments about whose turn it is to clean and whose it isn't. And best of all, the work will get done *quickly*.

To clean as well as a team, you need a good coach or manager to set things up, just as in any other team sport. In your home, *you* get to be the coach (even if you are a working coach). Everyone doesn't just grab a cloth or sponge and start cleaning. Instead, you assign specific duties to each person on the team, as each person will be doing a different job in the same location. One dumps all trash while another dusts or spot cleans, or one does the insides of windows and the other the outsides. After all the tasks are divvied up, the gang starts in on the target area and everyone completes assignments as swiftly as possible. Then the coach makes a quick inspection to ensure quality before everyone moves on.

The secret of successful team cleaning is a little bit of planning before you begin. Just as in a football play, everyone has a job to do, a time to do it, and a way to move to get it done. Huddle with your kids: "Okay guys, here's the play. We're going to hit the living room. We'll start at the right of the door as we go in. Matt, you take this sack and pick up all the trash. Work to your left around the room till you get back to the door. Then place the trash bag outside the door. I'll move in after Matt and do the high dusting with this lambs' wool duster and work my way around the room hitting cobwebs, the top of the bookshelves, lamps, high corners, the top of the valances, and anything else above six feet. Jenny, you follow me, doing the flat surfaces with this treated dust cloth, hitting everything below six feet, including the legs of furniture and chairs. Matt, as soon as you're done trashing, go back in and help Jenny dust, but you start on the left side of the door and work your way back until you and Jenny meet. I'll follow you guys with a vacuum and by the time you're finished, I should be close behind. I'll make sure we didn't miss anything while you go on and start the dining room. Any questions? Remember, we want to move fast but get the job done well. We've got the number-one team in town, so let's get going."

When it's time to do a thorough cleaning, one person can move the furniture out and back and another can vacuum. Or when you do high cleaning, have someone at the foot of the ladder hand things up, saving the cleaner many trips up and down. When you wash walls or paint, it really speeds things up to have an extra pair of hands to help move heavy furniture, remove and replace decorations, go get the tool you forgot, and change water and towels when your hands are in the grime or paint.

Team cleaning makes people feel as if they're accomplishing something. If you make it a game and even a little bit of a competition, they'll hardly notice they're cleaning. This isn't magic, of course. You may still meet resistance. But when you work right along with the team, it helps a lot to motivate them.

Remember, this doesn't have to be done on the weekend. Forty-five minutes with a team some evening can clean any house so it'll never need to be touched on a weekend.

Being given responsibility for a single chore in every room—the "policer," the trasher, the vacuumer, the spot cleaner, the glass cleaner, the duster, or the straightener alone—enables an assignee to move quickly through the whole house without getting bored.

Even if you don't do your regular house cleanup this way, you might want to tackle a big or rush job—indoors or out—all together, and have some fun (such as a snowball fight) in the process.

Winning Teams

My readers have come up with some creative strategies to tackle the housework as a team. Some of their ideas for a game plan may work for you!

> "My family and I went through endless piles and mounds of single socks that had been carelessly accumulated from wash to wash, resulting in an unparalleled pile of unmated socks. We worked together as a family for hours and hours, hoping that maybe, just maybe, we could overcome this monster. We did!"

> "We found it most successful to have a designated time and day, usually weekly, when we did the major stuff—i.e., bathrooms, vacuuming, dusting, mopping—so that we were all working at the same time. That seemed to help all 'buy into' the process. Of course this gets harder as the children get older, but by then hopefully they are more responsible and can work on their own schedule."

> **"A chore chart might work for some, but we just designate a cleaning day, and that's an all-day, all-play event!"**

> "One thing that worked was Sunday night speed-cleaning. I'd announce that we were all going to clean for half an hour. Dad too. This was usually at the supper table. Then we'd have a discussion about what were the most noticeable dirt issues, divide them up, and just go at it for half an hour. When the time was up, we quit no matter where we were. It was usually a vast improvement. I'm an at-home mom, and the biggest issue was waking on Monday morning to the whole weekend's accumulated mess. This half-hour speed clean made a huge difference in the start of our week."

"My seventeen-year-old daughter recently joined a housekeeping crew. Though she's the youngest in the crew, she's the fastest. She attributes it to housecleaning sprints we do at home. I tell the kids, for instance, that we are going to clean the house in two hours. There are six of us, so we set the timer for twenty minutes, assign each person a section of the house, and see how much we can accomplish before the timer goes off. It's amazing what we can do, and the kids are so proud they usually want to have friends over afterwards."

"I have six girls, and everyone picks a room. Then we set a timer and try to make the biggest impact we can in fifteen minutes. I tell them we are halfway there at seven minutes. We all line up afterward and go through the house and each person gets to show off the room he or she cleaned. After all the showings we verbally vote on who made the biggest impact, and no one can vote for themselves. They love the timer because they know there is an end to this cleaning and they better work quickly if they want to win."

"Three out of four of the kids clean with us, and we divide things into a laundry-folding station, a sweeping/vacuuming station, a dusting station, and a dishes station. We add some fun thing, like getting Mario in first place on the video game. I set the timer for ten minutes, with one person at each station, including the video game. At the end of ten minutes, we switch to the next station. That way, I get to each task to make sure the details are done, and the youngest gets a try at the vacuum. I reset the timer as many times as there are participants, so we are done in less than an hour."

"Here's what I do when we need to clean the house fast. I ask the kids and my husband what their schedules are. I set a time and ask everyone to plan to be home at a certain time for one hour. Then we start the 'Family Clean.' We divide into two teams. My husband goes with one team, and I go with the other. We divide the house, assigning each team certain rooms and chores that need to be done. We can get the whole house done in one hour with everyone's help, and we do it together."

"When we team clean, we don't move off one level of the house until everything is done there. That way vacuums, brooms, cleaners, etc., move with us and we don't waste time looking for things."

"Once or twice a year, we take a week to deep clean the house together."

Teach Attitude, Too: Cleaning Is Part of Life

We need to extend "demonstration" beyond teaching the family how to clean and illustrating the skills of cleaning. The skills of cleaning are not hard to teach—cleaning includes a lot of picking up and hanging up, which any second grader can easily do, plus some sweeping, spraying, and wiping. A lot of it is no-brain procedures. Anyone can learn to pick up, straighten up, clean a spot off a wall, or plug in a vacuum.

The key here is transferring these skills into an attitude and habit as consistent as breathing. Instead of trying to make time for cleaning or squeeze it into our schedule—set aside a day or afternoon for it—we must demonstrate that cleaning is a natural part of life. It's an automatic act and a responsibility that flows into and is built into everything you do.

Cleaning should be thought of as an everyday, ongoing process like walking, talking, breathing, or eating. We have forever singled it out as a function separate from life, turning cleaning into an event, a ceremony—"Hold everything, men and women, it's time to clean." Few people, when making plans, include a consideration of how much mess the event at hand may cause. We just go for it, and then, after we have "enjoyed life," we survey the mess and plan a later attack for getting things clean. But the cleanup should be part of the party. In short, we shouldn't have to stop life to clean up, or wait until we can't wade through the mess and then take a day to restore things. Cleaning should be part of every day and hour so there is no separate "cleaning time."

You can encourage this important attitude best by having everything needed to clean conveniently available, having your home free of junk and clutter, and having it furnished as far as possible to resist soil and stains and make cleaning easy. Talking about and planning for the cleanup when you're setting up anything is another way to make cleaning part of life instead of something you take time out of life to do.

Many failures to clean up happen not because somebody didn't know how, but because the person simply didn't include it in their thinking. It's easy to teach cleaning methods and mechanics—the secret is getting cleaning laced into life.

Bring the "Why" of Cleaning to Life

Sometimes we focus so keenly on the mechanical, physical aspects of cleaning that we lose the idea of *why* we are doing it and what it means to live in a nice orderly environment.

One of the best ways to reinforce the value of clean is to constantly, in front of everyone, express how wonderful it is to be clean, and live in a clean house, with clean clothes, clean food, clean air, a clean car, and clean yard. This will do a lot to bring the "why" of cleaning to life.

The Constant Cleaning Tour

There are cleaning demonstrations going on all of the time, all over the place, so when you are with the family, don't fail to take advantage of them. Disneyland, for example, is one of the most inspirational examples around. It is always clean (and being cleaned), and the people doing it are sharp and friendly. Make sure you comment on this, stop to watch, and relate the cleanliness to the good time you are all having. This makes cleaning part of that good time.

The more you can point out the benefits and pleasures of cleanliness, the more positive carryover you'll get for kids to clean at home. When you're at a sharp, clean place like a beautiful park or handsome hotel, say, "Look how clean this place is. Isn't it great, doesn't it make you feel good?" Or "This is sure a nice clean restaurant." Or "Let's stop at this service station; it's cleaner." Things like this are a powerful influence for kids to adopt "clean" as an ethic and behavior in their lives.

Keep your eye out for the janitors, maids, litter pickers, and window cleaners always doing something somewhere, and you can all observe both the skills involved here and the results, right before your eyes. Take advantage of any demonstration you can find, and be sure to talk to the people involved. "How do you do that?" Most people are proud and eager to tell you about their work.

Reinforce the Value of "Clean"

Likewise, never fail to point out messy, filthy, or disorderly things when you're driving or walking through the countryside, town, park, or anywhere! When you see something like this, ask your kids to look at it and sadly say how ugly it is. Talk about how bad it makes you feel or how anyone who passes by or lives there must feel.

Take your kids on community cleanup-day projects. It can have a profound effect on their attitude toward mess creation. After they police the litter from a street gutter or five-mile stretch of highway, their chances of chucking something out the window of a car are small. And this will carry over to their room, home, and yard. Most of the people who come to such events are thoroughly converted to keeping America or the community beautiful, and this reinforces values as well.

> "I try to teach my kids how much nicer a neat home is than a messy one. We talk about how much easier it is to find toys or favorite clothes when they're put away. We also talk about how good a clean home looks and feels and smells, and how we can all help by putting our own things away and picking up after ourselves. When it's all neat, I ask them to look around and see how everything is put away, and I ask them if they feel happier because the house is clean."

One Last Note

The mothers of the past usually spent more time teaching girls to clean than boys. To help bring about the cleaning revolution, be careful not to do that.

> "I have one daughter and three sons. When they were born I inspected their hands and found out that there was no difference in them so they all had to learn the same things."

> "My two boys learned to clean, wash, iron, sew buttons, and to cook as well as my daughter and me. They are married now and share housework equally with their working wives. I am so proud of them!"

> "I even had the kids sew on their own loose buttons. Threading a needle requires dexterity, and pride in successfully accomplishing the task was apparent. I knew if the boys were bachelors for any length of time, they would be glad they knew how to reattach buttons and make minor clothing repairs."

Chapter 12

The Good, the Bad, and the Ugly: Three Child Cleanup Challenges for Parents

This chapter concentrates on three subjects within the topic of child cleanup that deserve some extra discussion: teaching the very youngest children to clean (fun and easy!); instilling cleaning habits in teens (often hard!); and getting kids to keep their rooms clean (always hard!)

The Biggest Secret: Starting Young!

One bit of advice that successful parents of "all-cleaning families" repeat over and over is that kids are never too young to start cleaning. Human beings are infinitely moldable—as any number of famous sayings note, from "As the twig is bent, so grows the tree" to "Train up a child in the way he should go, and when he is old he will not depart from it." Put this fact to the service of good by training children young to love cleaning.

If you don't let children start cleaning during the early years, when they want to, you'll be in for a very difficult reconversion process by the time they're bigger. That's when suddenly *we* want them to clean, and getting them to go along is a struggle.

The younger they are, the more they want to please.

"If you start young enough, kids just understand they are expected to help out."

The process begins, of course, by letting kids clean up after *themselves*. By the time a child can understand simple directions, he or she can put stuffed animals and rubber balls back in the toy box.

As your children's toys get more advanced, so do the chores. The toddler who puts toys back in the toy box grows into the preteen who puts the bicycle back in the garage at the end of the day—and who even occasionally takes the garbage cans to the curb without being asked!

"You can enable your children to be accomplished, or you can enable them to be lazy. It all depends on how you handle them when they are young."

Be careful when pigeonholing jobs as suitable for "big people" or "little people." As many parents have discovered (surprise, surprise!) even toddlers can pick up and put back. The biggest thrill and self-esteem builder I had as a boy was when one of my parents, uncles, teachers, or grandparents said, "Here, take over—you do it!" and handed me any of the following: the reins of a team of horses; the steering wheel of a massive truck; the handle to the "squeeze chute" we used to inoculate cattle; the paintbrush; the grain-sack sewing needle; the paste wax cloth; or the cattle counter. I did "big people's" jobs when I was six, seven, and eight. My family's confidence in me made me proud of the work, no matter what it was.

To a small child, everything is a toy. All the things you use as you go about your daily routine have a power of fascination for a child. They want to try that "game" of pushing that machine or broom across the floor; they want to rub that soft cloth across the end table, too.

When they're at this young, enthusiastic stage, you can buy them their own small cleaning tools (as described in Chapter 8). You can either let them pretend while you do the real thing or let them work right along with you. During the toddler years, take some of the cleaning activities and make a game of them. Low dusting, as we call it in my business, is ideal for toddlers. Give them a dust cloth or lambs' wool duster and have them race you in the job of dusting to a finish point. Three- and four-year-olds love to vacuum with a small hand-held vacuum, so let them go after the spilled potting soil or the crumbs under the kitchen table. Toddlers also like to shop. Let them use a wagon or toy shopping cart to go from room to room and "police"— the name we pros give the job of picking up the litter and left-behind things in an area before we vacuum.

Try to stick with sessions of no more than ten minutes so you can hold their interest, and keep the games fresh so they don't get bored. Give a prize or a treat when the game is finished.

Some Advice from the Moms and Dads of Our Youngest Cleaners

Some of my readers have been very successful in their efforts to start their children cleaning at a young age. Here are some of their methods for raising clean kids!

> "One of the keys to having kids help is to start early enough. Kids go through a time when they want to help, and this is the time to start."

"Get your kids excited about and involved in cleaning from as early an age as possible. My second-youngest son was choosing brooms when he was four."

"If children learn the habit of picking up after themselves early (and I'm talking age one), it will bless them for the remainder of their lives. It's much easier to train a toddler than to have to retrain a twelve-year-old who has been tossing her jacket on the floor for the past ten years."

"I start my children making their beds when they first get out of their crib and into a 'big' bed. One thing my kids fight over is washing dishes. They all love to play in the bubbles! Admittedly, my kids are young (six, five, three, and one), but if you start young, it gets easier as they get older."

"When my children ask to help with putting away the dishes, cooking, folding clothes, etc., I remind myself that although it would be so much easier and quicker to just do it myself, in a few years I'll want them to help! So I let them help now, even if it takes three times as long and makes a huge mess. "

Things Young Children Can Do

Of course, all young children require supervision while cleaning. Here are some jobs that are safe and helpful for your little ones to do!

"A three-year-old can dust the baseboards easier than a sixty-four-year-old. That child may not be as proficient, but practice can make perfect. There is a good reason to train children to be a part of the cleaning process as well as part of the mess process."

"I started teaching my children to clean and organize when they were very small—eighteen months old. Yes, really. A toddler can pick up his own toys, put his shoes in order on the closet floor, dust the legs of chairs, push a dust mop, put his socks together in his dresser drawer, fold washcloths, and even make his own bed (which at this stage consists of folding a blanket so Mommy can put it in the crib). In other words, get 'em used to it early. Build a habit so they do it automatically."

"When they were young, our children just worked alongside me and my husband. Whatever we were doing, we gave them part of it to do and then praised them for it. When they were three, they could shake the bathroom rugs or hold the dustpan or dust individual pieces of furniture or fold washcloths or set the spoons, etc."

"When the floor needs to be scrubbed, I let my three small children wash their plastic dishes. Then I follow up their job with mopping the floor."

"My three year old always wants to help me do anything. He is always saying 'Can I help, Mama? Can I help, Mama? Mama? MAMA???" It's enough to drive me crazy sometimes! I know I can always get the job done faster if he is not hanging around. But if I want him to make a long-term commitment to cleaning—and enjoying it—I have to let him start now."

"I let even the younger children know that if their friends are coming over, they have to help get the house ready. I have them use nontoxic cleaning products (even plain water or regular soap!) so that it's safe. Our new pastor and his family were coming over for dinner once. Their kids were the same age as my younger two, so my kids were excited. They actually FOUGHT over who got to clean the bathroom! When our company arrived, my four-year-old grabbed the pastor's hand and led him to our bathroom, telling him to 'look how pretty I cleaned the potty!' He is a great guy and was very enthusiastic with his praise for the girls."

Some How-to Pointers

Other parents of "can-do cleaners" also have good tips for getting kids to pitch in on the cleaning. Here are a few.

"As a mother of five, I know children must help. There are lots of ways to make this dream a reality. If you start when they are young, chores are a fun way of imitating the grownups and being BIG! And what child doesn't want to be big? I spray the tables and the little ones love to wipe it up."

"For younger children who can't read, a picture job chart is a great thing. We have drawings of how a bed looks when it's made and of clothes being put in the laundry chute on each of our girls' little job charts. When they see these, it reminds them of what they can do to help and how to do it."

"Start early (even if you have to rewash the dishes later). And be sure to make it a positive thing. Make it sound like it is a privilege to help Mommy or Daddy clean. Get excited about it. Even if they break a couple of dishes or miss a spot, don't discourage them or belittle their efforts."

"For younger children, especially, make tasks specific and measurable and not vague, as in 'Clean up your room.' You can use this to work on colors–'Pick up all the red things.' (This includes clothes, toys, books, etc.–anything red.) You can also work on counting–'Pick up five blocks.'"

"It seems to work better if I stay in my four-year-old's room while he is doing his chores. It takes longer to do it this way, because I could very easily go in his room and be finished in ten minutes, but I feel like I owe it to him to teach him things instead of sticking him in front of a television while I spend my day off cleaning the house."

"Work together at first. Tell them that this is play for grownups and that they may play with you. (The extra benefit is that you don't have to play Barbies or Candyland later, because you have already played together!"

"I don't know if you would call this manipulation, bribery, or positive reinforcement, but if one of the little ones starts to pick up her toys, I'll say, 'Oh, Sammy, you cleaned up your toys— you're so sweet!' I praise her and the others hear it and they want that praise too. They want the positive attention I'm giving the one who cleaned up."

"When I clean the bathroom my little ones join in with a spray bottle (with water only in it) and a cloth; they clean the door while I clean the toilet. You can have the little ones wear swimming goggles if they have trouble with which way round the spray bottle goes and it only makes it more fun! "

"My son wipes the counter in the children's bathroom. I bought a box of inexpensive, unscented baby wipes, and he takes a wipe, wipes the faucet, counter and sink, then tosses the wipe."

"When I'm cleaning the bath and shower, I have the little ones clean with me. I've even had them change into swimming clothes, stand on the bath mat, and have fun cleaning. I use dishwashing liquid and we make lots of bubbles."

"These little ones we may push aside because they are 'too little to really help' eventually lose this natural desire to be helpful. Eventually they will just give up. And these are the children who, when they grow up, have no idea how to vacuum, do dishes, or mop the floor because it was either never taught to them or never done 'to Mommy's satisfaction.' There are children, on the other hand, who are brought up with the attitude that they are very special and are good helpers (however insignificant the task). These are the ten-year-olds who are terrific moppers, vacuumers, and dishwashers. They actually enjoy helping out around the house and sometimes even cook better than their parents! They were lousy when they started at three but now are skilled enough to help make the house sparkle…"

Teen Cleaning

Those cute toddlers who followed us around with a toy broom as we cleaned have a way of growing into teenagers who wouldn't follow us anywhere! (Or at least anywhere their friends would see them.) Teens are into impressing people outside the home, so it can become harder to get their attention on those largely "invisible," purely intramural (read, "home") matters.

By the time your children reach even the preteen years, you've no doubt also noticed what *individuals* they're becoming. Time to readjust the chores (and occasionally, their timing and scheduling) to meet their individual needs! And no, don't worry that you'll fail to notice that they and their chore schedules and preferences (and skill levels) are changing—they will definitely let you know.

The teen years are no place to forget standards and expectations, however. If anything, you need to keep your guard up more than ever, as young people begin to take themselves more seriously . . . perhaps too seriously at times. Let me give an example from my own life.

A farmer's livestock is his lifeline, and when a birth occurs in the barnyard, everything is rescheduled around the care of the new arrival. Meals are interrupted, fishing trips canceled, dates delayed, bedtime ignored, and all personal needs and problems are put on hold until the animal is on its feet and feeling fine. Many unexpected wet, shivering new calves were carried into the house, dried and cleaned off by the stove, and then carefully placed back in the cozy barn on clean straw, and we only felt good about that. When you were working with a team of horses and stopped for any reason, you checked and patted your team, and when noon or night came you unhooked or unharnessed those horses, and then fed and watered them before you ate or drank anything yourself—that was the rule of the ranch, no exceptions.

I remember a moment of vanity in my teen years once, when I'd scored many heroic points at a ballgame, and my parents and I were applauded by many a friend and neighbor. The next night ball practice ran late, and though I usually hitched a ride for part of the six miles home, that night I walked and ran it all so instead of arriving home at 5:30 I came dragging in at almost 7:00. I was tired and famished and on the table Mom had left roast, mashed potatoes, fresh homemade bread, and raspberry jam. It was too much to pass up and I pulled up a chair to dig in. Suddenly Dad appeared at the door: "Have you fed your animals?" (Remember now, I'm a senior in high school, star athlete, student body president, his offspring, and on the brink of starvation.) "No, in a minute, Dad." "Why you lazy little snot," he said, yanking my chair from under me as I darted toward the back door, "No real man eats before his cows."

> "Early teenage. YIKES!!! Did anything work??? Oh yeah, 'If you do these chores you'll live another day'??? Just joking! Usually I gave the mom look and said, 'Do this and maybe later we can do blah blah' (something they might want to do). I always explained, even now, that they needed to do their part ('See moms can't do it all and work . . .'). Without their help we all suffer or lose precious time together that we can never get back. Believe it or not this actually works."

> "When children turn into teens, chores change. If children are running to school and jobs, it is hard for them to keep up on it all. So we just flex a little. For example, I am willing to put clothes in the dryer for one of our sons when he has done most of his part and just needs some sleep. So I switch laundry for him, and in the morning he takes his dry laundry to his room. In the big picture he really helps me, himself, and we help each other! I think family cooperation is the key to chores."

"When our son was in high school and busy with sports and studies, we negotiated a slight reduction in his list of chores and he negotiated that he do 90 percent of the chores on the weekend or on days when he didn't have practices, games, and lots of homework. He discovered how much he could get done in increments of ten minutes or less, and the number of chores on his list was never an issue."

"When the children were elementary age, I gave them a schedule with only a few jobs a day. Now, they choose their own schedule, doing most of the cleaning from Thursday to Saturday. If someone has a busy week or will be gone over the weekend, there are certain jobs that can wait until next week (but not the bathrooms!)."

"I usually worked with the kids, but when they got into junior high I would leave them to clean while I went to the grocery store. Then it was a race to be done before I got home and I would reward them with Burger King or pizza for dinner. They always seemed to do a superb job and I got my house cleaned for about $20 (cheap!) and without the grumbling."

"I am a Girl Scout leader with a group of Cadettes, girls who are preteen or in their early teens. We made cookies last week and really had a mess when they were done. A lot of girls this age just want to talk and visit—they're hard to motivate to clean up. But you usually have one or two who will start to clean up when you ask them."

"Whoever starts to clean up, I say something like, 'Oh, Ashley, you're my favorite—but don't tell anybody!' And then I give her a hug. I'm laughing when I say it, but the other girls hear it and they want a hug and praise too and will usually start to help. Girls this age still seem to always want to be the favorite with the leader."

"When kids get to teenage status, encourage them to have a friend over to clean with them. I have done this with my kids, and they LOVE to see and clean each other's mess. It's entertaining, active, and friendship-binding because they are helping each other. Good alternative once they outgrow working with the adult in the household."

"Since my older girls like to take long showers on occasion, that's when you could have them use soap scum remover on the shower doors and clean the shower all over while they are in there."

"My daughter is thankful she knows how to keep things clean. She was able to spend a summer at age seventeen with two of her best friends . . . working a part-time job while sharing an apartment in a roommate situation. She found she was keeping it all clean and they were depending on her. 'Wow, Mom,' she said, 'Now I know how you felt some days when we didn't want to do chores.' One day she went on strike and the others said, 'Oh Audrey, you aren't doing the dishes anymore!' She said, 'No, not til you start doing them too.' Then they all began doing chores together; it was a learning experience for all. My daughter is more prepared for marriage and being a college roommate from this experience."

"To get my high school-age son to help clean I use this analogy: The way you practice is the way you play. Football practice is designed to build good playing habits and skills. Coaches make you practice to help you be your best. Likewise, your years as a teenager are actually practice years for the 'big game' when you are an adult. Your parents are the coaches. How do you want to play in the big game? Will your house and clothes be neat and tidy when you are an adult? Or sloppy?"

Room Control

Children and teenagers are often willing to do their share of general household cleaning, the laundry, the yard work, and overall clutter control, but they have the attitude "My room is exempt" from the family's cleanliness standards.

Yes, it *is* their space, but it's in your family's home. Their rooms may not be as visible as a well-manicured front lawn or even a dust-free living room, but they are part of the home too, not just a catch-all for everything they personally don't want to wash, sort, file, hang up, throw away, or put away.

In most children's rooms, clutter can be a bigger problem than cleaning (as described in Chapter 3).

Family Circle recently ran a national "Win a Trip to Hawaii" contest, in which entrants submitted a ten-minute video displaying their clutter. It was interesting how often, after showing all of their own junk and clutter, they would at the end of the video often go into their kids' rooms and say, "Now look at this mess these mini packrats have here." Beware! Kids will often conform to we adults' expectations and example, whether good or bad.

Don't ever let up or just give up and say, "It's your mess, you live in it." It isn't just their mess as long as society (that is, the rest of the family) is around. There is no inborn right to be trashy, at home or in Mother Nature at large.

In children's rooms or for any other cleaning tasks, you also want to avoid drastic up-and-down swings in which the area goes from "disaster" to "delightful." This a super damaging pattern to set. It will carry over into other behavior: let your teeth rot, then try to repair them; let the car grind to a stop, then try to get it going again; let the heart attack happen, then go see the doctor. When restoration is too big, a job ambition decreases or disappears. Living in a mess for even one hour is too much; living in a mess for a month inflicts psychological damage in the acceptance of the idea that it is okay to mess up because "someday" you can clean up. Many of those "big cleanup later" times never come or a lot of damage has been done before they do.

> "We clean homes, and some of our customers tell us to skip their kid's room because it is too messy—we try to open the door to look at it and can't even see where the floor is. We find so much rotting food in rooms it is terrible. I saw a bed today that had nine sheets on it! Instead of the teenager taking off the soiled sheet each time he would just put another on top!"

> "I've tried letting their rooms go to the point that they should have been disgusted by their own filth and cleaned up without being asked. That definitely didn't work, as I realized when I pulled moldy food out from under the bed and found ants in a drawer!!!!"

The Messy Rebellion Period

Kids are always in imminent danger of entering the messy rebellion period, or MRP. In other words, they are liable to suddenly begin leaving their rooms a mess on purpose, indefinitely. Kids love privileges, so instead of grounding them in their room until they clean it or trying to wait them out, say "When your room is ready you can go to your friend's house," or whatever the teen's desire might be. Kids can be stubborn, but they do depend on parents for privileges, money, and transportation, so you hold the power. It might take some pressure tactics at first, but kids learn fast.

You can also go to their room and start cleaning it slowly, very slowly. They will get disgusted watching you take forever and will soon "show you how to do it faster and better." So do that puttering-around act well! Teenagers, especially, hate to have Mom clean their rooms.

Whatever you do, don't say, "This is your room and you are solely responsible for it." This takes away your authority. They will counter by saying, "Well, if it's my room I can keep it the way I want!" Tell them instead, "This is one of the rooms in our house, and you are using it. You know how we keep our house and how you have to keep this room."

Teach the Principle of "Keep Up" Cleaning

We often get so focused on getting the room cleaned that we forget that *keeping* it clean is just as important to the overall success of child cleaning. Keeping a room up every morning or evening is only a bit of work, and it's much easier to take than a big, long session of cleaning every so often. Once kids get the picture, they are usually converted to "keep up" cleaning faster than most adults.

> "Before they go to bed, the kids have to pick up their room, and there cannot be anything left on the floor. Anything they don't know what to do with is placed on their bedroom chair. This accomplishes a few things. It creates a habit by making cleaning part of their bedtime routine; it helps me to see what items don't have a designated place by what is routinely left on the chair; and lastly it helps keep the room uncluttered, making it simpler to actually clean later."

**Dear Young Cleaners,**

Your room is your own personal little kingdom, after all—you should take full charge of it.

So clean it up and keep it clean—floor, dresser tops, tables, shelves, drawers, closets, and windows. Kill those cobwebs, and keep your toys and trinkets neat. Set the pictures straight, and make the bed. Keep your room as clean as a whistle, so no one ever has to come in and force you to do it, or do it for you.

Your friend,

Don Aslett

Other Thoughts and Solutions

"The kids I know whose parents treat the child's room as off limits have kids who learn to live in appalling messes. Even for the teens in our home, tidying up for cleaning day was never optional and involved me being in the room if needed. I don't see why we should allow any part of our house to be a disaster area, and I don't think it teaches basic standards for caring for their own stuff."

"First, my room has to be clean and decluttered. How can I make them clean their room when mine is the laundry dump, or where we stuffed all the boxes of junk when company was coming? We need to set the example so the kids will have a clean room to copy."

"I discovered early on that the worst thing to tell a child is 'go clean your room.' They have no clue where to even start, so they simply sit down and start playing with anything that is handy. I found if I made a little list, things got done a lot faster. Make your bed; pick up your clothes and put them in the hamper; pick up toys on the floor and put them in the toy box; hang your coat in the closet; put your shoes neatly in the closet, etc. Children seem to work better when given a specific task to do—not something as general as 'clean your room.'"

Be Prepared for the Excuses!

"It doesn't look dirty to me."
"Does it look clean to you?"
"Grant's room is worse than this."
"Grant doesn't live here."
"It's my room, isn't it? Why do you care what it looks like?"
"You're right, it is your room. But it's our house."
"If I clean up, I won't be able to find anything."
"Once you clean up, I'll help you find anything you've misplaced."
"I already cleaned it up! You should have seen it before."
"Less dirty doesn't necessarily mean clean."

"1. Establish ownership. What they care for, they can redecorate or design if they keep it clean. 2. Get a small vacuum cleaner for their bedroom that is easier to handle. I have a little Europro or the Mighty Mite by Eureka. My girls are seven and ten now. 3. Use bins to store their belongings. My girls labeled and arranged their own bins: hair, toys, devotions, writing, art and crafts, etc."

"I recently stumbled upon a better way of before-bedtime toy pickup. I have two girls, ages four and seven, who share a room. By the end of the day, the room can look like a hurricane came crashing through. When they were told to pick up together, they would do more playing than picking up. So I separate them–send one off for a light bedtime snack while the other works, then vice versa. This seems to do the trick!"

"Children's rooms constantly need cleaning, dusting, and decluttering, but if kids are constantly harassed to clean, they feel like they live in a glass house and can't ever just let their hair down and enjoy life. The solution is simple. Teach them that they have to straighten up their rooms at only two specific times: The first is when they get ready for bed. I taught my kids that they have to 'put their room to bed' as well as their body. So, in addition to brushing their teeth and changing into pajamas, they clean up their room. This way they never have to wake up to yesterday's mess. They wake to a clean slate.

"The second time to straighten up is whenever you leave the house for any reason. For example, if they are leaving for a date, their room has to be in order first. Don't ask me why these two simple rules have worked so well, but they have."

"The kids' bedrooms are no trouble because they clean them or lose them. Sounds tough, but although they love sleeping with each other, they want their own rooms and guard that personal space with cleaning care. (We don't expect the moon but do want basic clutter controls, daily wipe-downs of some things, and deeper cleaning at times, such as every couple weeks.) The list of what Mom and Dad think is a clean room is posted (the youngest has a photograph of the clean room hanging, too) so there is no unknown. We inspect, and they beam, 'Come see what I did.'"

"If my kids don't keep their rooms clean, I put a grade on the door from A to F—that helps most of the time."

"I told my ten-year-old daughter that we would redo her room, but she would have to keep it clean. Instead of doing the makeover all at once—quilt, curtains, paint, rugs—we're changing it little by little. I bought her the quilt but did not buy the matching curtains until the next week, and she had to keep her room clean that week. One of the first things I bought for her room was a matching laundry basket in the new color and told her she would have to keep her clothes picked up and in it if she wanted the other makeover things. If she doesn't keep her room clean, then we won't buy the next thing on the makeover list."

"When my two girls were small I got desperate for help, so one day I gave them a half hour to get their laundry picked up, toys put away, beds made, and so on. The half hour went by and they did not move. So, I opened the door to the outside, got a broom, and started sweeping everything that was on the floor out the door. They scrambled to save their toys, books, and clothing. The threat of this happening again got results with their help for about a year. Eventually I quit nagging, closed their bedroom doors when company came, and when they had a sleepover it was their responsibility to explain what happened to the room."

The Teen Room Challenge

"As teenagers they may resist keeping their room clean. Let them have control over their own room, simply close the door. Respect their need to be individuals; this is a time they may choose not to do things like Mom and Dad. There are more important battles to be won at this age. If you have already taught them the skills at a young age, don't worry, they will still remember them when they leave the teen years and return to a clean, organized environment."

"Teenagers' rooms are tougher. Tell 'em clean your room or I'll do it for you. If you plan to send them off to camp, give them a week's warning that their room needs to be clean before they go. After you send them off, go clean their room. Depending on the level of the ... ahem ... difficulty, you can elect to just pitch a lot of things; or bag them up and put them in the garage to be sorted when they get home. The trick to that is to make sure they do the sorting out in the garage! It sounds brutal, but I really did just throw a lot of junk away while they were gone. And when they came home you know what they said? They said, 'Wow, Mom, you cleaned our room, it looks really nice!' They never once missed anything. Sometimes the amount of stuff just gets overwhelming for kids; they are grateful when someone gets in there and helps them. I used to try and do this sorting with them, it seemed more democratic, but we never got anywhere. So the camp thing was born out of desperation."

"Our teenage daughter's room was always a mess, and clothes seemed to be the biggest problem. There were always clothes all over the floor and the furniture, as she tossed things down when she took them off or flung them around while looking for a certain outfit. One day we said to her, 'It seems that you have too many clothes, and if we reduce the number it would probably really help you out. You pick out three of everything, and we'll put the rest away for a while.' So she did, and we packed all of the rest up in clean garbage bags and tucked them away. (We figured that before long the embarrassment of wearing the same outfits over and over would get to her, and she'd be more likely to appreciate all she had and take better care of it.) She toughed it out through all of three weeks before she finally asked if she could have some of her other clothes back, and it did effect a reformation, at least for a while."

"One thing, when they were teenagers, that always worked: after their bedrooms had turned into fetid pits of garbage, dirty clothes strewn among the clean ones, crumpled papers, torn magazines, and possibly deceased small animals, my husband, out of desperation, came up with a solution. He would say, 'You've got thirty minutes to clean your rooms or I'm taking your doors off the hinges.' They didn't believe him at first, but he DID IT. For a teenager, having no bedroom door was unbearable, and they would, finally, clean their rooms, weeping and moaning about their cruel parents. When it was really, really clean (dusted, vacuumed, several garbage bags filled and placed in the garage), Dad would replace their doors. I don't know of anyone else who has tried this. It worked, though. The threat and carrying out of the door removal worked only when it came from their dad. This was always a last-ditch measure."

Chapter 13

It's Not Enough to Just "Hang the Chart": Follow Up!

The packed van pulled into the only remaining campsite. Four youngsters leaped from the vehicle and began feverishly unloading gear and setting up a tent. The boys then rushed off to gather firewood, while the girls and their mother set up the camp stove and cooking utensils. A nearby camper marveled to the youngsters' father, "That, Sir, is some display of teamwork." "I have a system," the father replied. "No one goes to the bathroom until the camp is set up."

After introducing our children to the idea of helping to clean, doing our best to motivate them, dividing the chores, and teaching them how to clean, we reach the inevitable stage of enforcing whatever plan or arrangement we have made with them. This is in many respects the trickiest and most important step of all.

Today's parents often want to be their child's best friend; we want the time we do have with our children to be friendly and nonconfrontational. This can pose a problem when the time comes to see that things are carried out. It's been said that the first law of heaven is obedience—for sure it is a necessary law in the home. As I said earlier, the same behavior children display in care and cleaning will carry into all of their other behavior patterns. Holding someone's feet to the fire when it comes to their share of cleaning chores will keep your family members from getting burned somewhere down the line, ten or twenty or forty years later in their lives.

Our children need to understand that when those in authority (or the majority) decide and make the rules. They have one option, especially when they are living at home: obey.

Think your enforcements plans and policies through, and discuss them with the family if possible. Get their ideas for the consequences of not keeping cleaning commitments. Then take a good, firm position so you don't have to keep making amendments to your resolutions.

> "What I have found most effective: Be consistent. These chores must be done regularly, and the kids will not get out of them by whining or complaining."

> "Through trial and error I figured out what did and didn't work. I came to realize that consistency needed to be top priority. Children need to know what their boundaries are! And if they don't do the expected task, there will be a consequence. If you are consistent, it really doesn't matter what the consequence is. The very fact that you followed through and did something will let them know that you mean business."

"One of the key phrases we repeat (and repeat) at our house is 'responsibilities before privileges.' If the kids ask to do something fun and we know they've left tasks undone, we simply say 'responsibilities before privileges' and they know to get busy."

Make Them Live the Consequences

Few of us like to hear that troublesome word "if," but it is there to deal with. If we do or don't do something there will be results that we own. One of the best ways to enforce the need for cleaning is to get kids to see the real-life consequences of not doing something.

"Make sure they realize the importance of the task at hand. Be willing to let them live with the consequences if they don't do the chore (no clean laundry if hamper is empty)."

"My youngest daughter's responsibility was to empty the dishwasher and put away the clean dishes. She hated to touch dirty dishes and after some negotiation, it was decided that each family member would rinse his or her own dishes and place them in the dishwasher after eating. If my daughter did not empty the dishwasher, the rest of us could not put our dishes in the machine and so they went in the sink. Because she was the cause of dishes in the sink, she then had to put away the clean dishes and load the dirty dishes.

"One week she tested the limits—after five days the dishes were overflowing the sink and counter tops. We were running out of silverware and cooking utensils, but I was NOT going to give in and do her work. That night I said to my husband, 'There aren't any more dishes to eat from or cook with. I guess we need to go out to dinner.' My daughter went to get her coat and was told that she would not accompany us because it was due to her negligence (and stubbornness) that there were no dishes. She needed to take care of the mess. All of it. She stayed home, did dishes until about eleven at night, and never again neglected her responsibility for that job. Moral: don't give in, and make the consequences so aversive the kid doesn't want to go there again."

"We have direct consequences for not completing chores in a timely manner. This is different for each child. I have one who could be grounded in his room all day and it would not really make much of an impact. He tends to be solitary by nature. I have another (my social butterfly) who would consider spending the day in her room to be cruel and unusual punishment. Another of our children loses the privilege to use anything electronic (TV, Nintendo, etc.). Consequences for disobedience (which is the real issue here) must be tailored to the child."

Enforcement Strategies

As we all know, it's not enough to set up a cleaning system or even to figure out consequences for when jobs are left undone. You must be ready with ways to motivate your workers and enforce the good cleaning habits you're trying to establish. The following sections provide a few pointers.

Set a Time Limit

I hate deadlines myself, but many parents have found them an effective way to make sure things get done.

> "Tell them what needs to be done, and give a deadline. This allows them some flexibility in their schedule and some say in the matter so they feel they have some control over the chore. If the job is not done by the deadline, then you must impose consequences. In our house, if my son leaves for school without making his bed and cleaning up his room, then he does not get to go to the gym to work out after school that day. Be sure the consequence is immediate and that you can easily enforce it."

> "Kids will be highly motivated to finish their chores if they have an activity planned or if mealtime is just on the horizon, and they risk being late for either if chores are not completed. Stick to your guns, and be consistent."

Take Away Privileges

> "I have to admit I tried just about everything to get my children to help around the house. I tried rewarding them. I tried grounding them. I tried scaring them with the fact that a dirty house invites dirty visitors such as ants and mice. I tried being the cleaning warden and saying things like, 'As long as you live under this roof you will clean what I tell you to clean.' But nothing seemed to work. I finally decided that I had to make the consequences of not doing the chores for them as important as doing the chores was for me. I thought hard about this and finally realized that my children were 'couch potatoes in training' and that television was the trick. Television rules have changed in our home now. The two older girls now get one hour of 'free' television a day. If they want to earn more television, they have to complete their chores daily and completely."

"We have a 'business before pleasure' rule that works well for daily chores. When my son gets home from school, there can be no 'screen time' of any kind until the table is set and the cat is fed."

"Punishment means taking away something they value. No dance on Friday, no sleepover, etc. While this is painful for both them and you (because you have to listen to them whine and complain), you only have to enforce this once or twice and your kids will know you mean business."

"When my daughter asks, 'Mom can I go here or there or can a friend stay over or can we go here or there,' I say 'Have you done your part?' And then I do a rundown. If any answer is 'no' then I say no."

"We have actually been using the verse from the Bible that basically states, (paraphrased) 'If you don't work, you don't eat.' I know that there are some who would go ballistic at that thought, but it is a great motivator at breakfast time to make beds and pick up the floor."

Charge 'Em

Although the value of a clean house should be motivation enough to keep up with housework, for children, sometimes it takes more to get them going.

"Our children get paid if they have their chores done by a certain time without being asked or continually reminded. The 'not asking or reminding' is crucial because the idea is for them to be responsible and accountable if they want to get their allowance. I will not fight or nag them. Depending on the child's age, one reminder at the beginning of the day or when they come home from school is fine, but by bedtime, if it isn't done, then I will dock their pay. After this happens they will see how serious I am."

Advice from the Scouts

"It comes down to this with Scouts: if you want to do this again, you need to do what I say. We don't have to let you do anything. If you want to go camping, but won't do your camp chores, we don't have to let you go camping next time. It's as simple as this: we don't have to let you participate. Adults in leader training are taught to stick to their guns. A child can see through empty threats. 'I'll wring your neck if you don't clean your room' defies common sense. Kids know you're not likely to do it. Kids, just like us, can tell empty threats from real ones. Everybody does their camping chores when we're camping, and when it's your turn to do dishes, you have to do them. Kids say, 'I don't have to dishes at home,' and I say, 'You're not at home.' They say, 'We have a dishwasher at home,' and I laugh and say, 'Yeah, it's probably a self-loading one, and the self-loader is your mom. If you don't want to wash the dishes, I won't wash them for you. You'll wash them or you can't come camping with us again.' Telling kids, 'You can't go camping again' has to mean you can't go camping again. And telling them they can't go to the movie if they don't mow the yard has to mean just that. Don't fall into the parent trap of, 'It's easier to do it myself than to get them to do it.' And if you start yelling at them, you have absolutely nowhere to go in the conversation."

–a longtime Boy Scout leader

"Clothes left on the floor, drawers, doors left open, lights left on . . . charge for these and deduct from allowance."

"I hired a housecleaner and told my two kids if they didn't keep their rooms clean and their stuff picked up, I would let the housecleaner go, and then they would have to do all that she does. That has worked the best. I also charge them $1 for each piece of clothing left on the floor of their rooms."

"When my kids were younger, I got tired of nagging them to keep their rooms and bathroom clean and to remember their chores. I work from home so it would bug me all day while they were at school when they left clothes, toys, etc., lying all around the house. I would inevitably end up picking them up so I wouldn't have to look at them. Not a good thing. So I typed up a price list for what it would cost them for their maid to pick up after them, gather dirty clothes, do chores they forgot, etc. I got little ticket books for each child and each morning after they left for school, I went through the house picking up like I always did, but I also wrote down in their ticket book the charge for what I had done for them that day. Once a week when I gave them their allowance, I also gave them a bill that had to be paid on the spot. It didn't take them long to realize that it was easier to do the little I expected of them than pay for maid service. On the price sheet, I also listed all the things that I do for them for no charge (laundry, taxi service, meal planning and preparation, etc.). I tried to keep it lighthearted while still making a point. I didn't have to do this for too long before they got it and things ran much more smoothly."

Confiscation Capers

Children, like us, are very protective of their belongings. Sometimes, the possibility of their belongings "disappearing" is enough motivation to clean them up.

"The maid bag. I warn my children that I'm going to go through the family room, and anything out of place or that does not belong there will be put in my maid bag. My maid bag is a large garbage bag. I go through the room and dump toys, odd socks, bracelets, notes for a term paper, their favorite book, etc., in the bag. Later, if my children miss an item, they can pay me a quarter to be able to look inside the bag to see if their missing item is there. If they want it out, they must work for it, usually an hour helping me. My oldest son, now a dad of six, still came home the weekend I threatened to clean out the part of the basement where he had things stored. He was afraid his things would end up in my maid bag!"

"After failing at many systems (charts, gold stars, threats, etc.), I tried one that worked like magic for the problem of all of us leaving stuff around and not putting it away. We called our game Confiscation. Each of us was allowed to declare a Confiscation Alert once each day, when everyone would run around putting sticky dots on items left out by others. Each person's stuff got a certain color dot, including my stuff! Then we collected the items in a laundry basket. Once there were fifty items! Items could only be reclaimed by paying twenty-five cents per item into a glass jar. Many times people decided the items weren't worth a quarter to them, and they abandoned them or threw them away, so that was an efficient way to declutter. I took the stickers off the items and put them in a notebook. I also paid into the system! I was the worst offender, so the kids really enjoyed 'catching' me. At the end of the week, we counted the stickers on each person's page and had a first- and second-place winner who divided the money."

"When my kids were little, I hated them leaving toys and clutter lying around, and I got tired of nagging. I would ask them once to pick their stuff up, and then after a certain amount of time (an hour for example) I would go and pick up what was still out and put it in a laundry basket. This was quick and easy because I didn't put any of it away. It would be confiscated for one week, and then they could get it back and put it away. When they were a bit older and had allowances they would have to pay to get the item out of impoundment! Some of this stuff they didn't even care about, so they didn't claim it even after a month—then I knew I could get rid of it. This system worked the best for me because there was no nagging involved."

Other Parental Penalties

"If the kids get a little lazy and slop through their chores—or don't do them at all—then the chore that wasn't done plus an additional household chore has to be done that day by them. The extra chore I get them to do is always one of the ones we put off until we 'have' to do them (like the closet under the stairs, the mudroom, or the laundry room). If they really have an attitude they get to sort all the unmatched socks (with our size family that is a BIG job!!)."

"The thing that's always bugged me the most about kids helping is all the whining about it, instead of just doing the next thing and getting it over with. We have the rule that if you fuss about having to do something, and/or complain about being bored, you get the pleasure of having another cleaning job assigned to you. With each protest, another job is assigned, until said protests cease and desist. (I think the record at our house was five). New children in our neighborhood are forewarned to never complain about being bored at our house, as I will gleefully head for the cleaning products."

"Snow shoveling was split between our boys, although when our younger son was arguing over who was to shovel what part of the driveway, my husband told him he could shovel the whole driveway by himself for the whole next month. Unfortunately for Kyle, it snowed every day that next month!! But, he never complained again about shoveling."

"Once, when my daughter was grumbling about having to unload the dishwasher, I said she had to wash the next meal's dishes, rinse them, dry them all by hand, and put them away. Somehow, unloading the dishwasher was never the burden she'd thought it was after that!"

"Make it more work not to do the chores rather than to do them. One day my older two girls whined incessantly about cleaning their bathroom. 'Mom, this is going to take two hours.' After growing weary of the complaining I sat them both down in the bathroom and said, 'Okay, I will clean it and you will time how long it takes and watch exactly how I do it.' (I had previously estimated for them that this was a thirty-minute project, or fifteen minutes apiece). After five minutes they were begging to do the chore themselves. But I said, 'No, you must watch, since this is so hard for you and will take so long.' After 10 minutes one said to the other, 'We could have already been out of here by now if we had done it ourselves.' So . . . make not doing the chore more painful than doing it."

Things NOT to Do to Young Cleaners

Threats are the most common and least effective tactic parents use to get children to be responsible. Instead of saying "You must" or "You better," stay calm. Yelling only leads to more yelling. Make it clear to your kids that they haven't lived up to expectation and that you're disappointed, but try not to be the heavy. You can even use humor to make the point.

Dealing with Stalling

In pilot training, learning how to get a plane out of a stall is an important skill. It's just as important to know how to get kids out of a stall and into the toilet stall when it needs cleaning. When you set or demand a limit or deadline, they turn into clock watchers, and you have the bad guy burden of being a timekeeper and policeperson. Kids as a rule are too creative to be cornered, and they soon learn that the more time goes by, the less chance they will have to do it today.

Getting them started is the key to stopping stalling. Few kids will refuse to budge when Mom, Dad, or an older sibling grabs a couple of tools, leads them to the job, and starts right in with them. Work with them for ten or fifteen minutes, and then hand the job over to them. After a few times of this, they will get the idea that stalling doesn't work.

You can also help kids realize how much time they add to something by putting it off—how much harder it will be to do X after stalling for two days. In home care, the key is to continually tell and show others how "now" is better than "later." Don't do the hold-out battle with stallers—they will win!

> "Since we homeschool our girls, we have a great deal of flexibility in our schedule. We've found it helpful to print out a 'morning chore chart' on our computer, with each girl's name and the list of things she needs to accomplish that morning before starting school. We also put a time when they need to be finished, to discourage dawdling. Each girl places a checkmark in the box when a chore is done, and, finally, she writes in the time she finishes. If a child consistently dawdles and finishes after the allotted time, she has to go to bed fifteen or thirty minutes earlier than usual, until the dawdling stops. (This usually only takes a day or two!)"

Inspecting

Prompt inspection has a threefold benefit. First, if the job is checked right away, it allows time for any quick corrections to be made. Second, it often ensures the job will be done. And third, it allows for quick feedback.

Nothing makes any of us—let alone a child—feel unappreciated more than to finish up a task and have no one notice. If you take the time to inspect, it shows your respect for their efforts.

Whenever possible, make your children a part of the inspection and evaluation process. Let them help set standards and help decide if something is clean or not.

"You've no doubt heard the maxim, 'Children do what you inspect, not what you expect.'"

"Always inspect the work; don't assume that it is being done."

"Follow up, follow up, follow up! When the kids tell me they're done, I ask them if it's ready to be inspected. Many times, they'll run back to do it a little better before inspection. In my experience, continue inspecting cleaning jobs indefinitely."

"After they have learned, it's also important to check their work periodically so you can see if they have forgotten how to do something or become lazy in how they are doing it."

"By far the hardest task is to go around and check up on the chores your children have done. For any system to work there must be accountability, and so you need to check to make sure things were done properly. It's amazing how easy it is to let this slip."

Stand Ready to Adjust Your Standards

Rather than requiring mates and kids to clean perfectly, our goal is to teach them "Clean is better than dirty." Our job is to inspire, expect, motivate them to take charge and enjoy cleaning. More perfect results can come later if we see fit. You must learn to tolerate mistakes by trainees: the sweater ruined in laundry, the floor with some dull and dirty patches, the wrong brand or size of something bought at the store.

"A lot of the problems I have with my nine-year-old son is that we have very different ideas of what constitutes 'clean.' We have had the most success when we have a clear and shared understanding from the beginning exactly what the criteria are on which cleanliness will be judged."

"Face it, the standard for a six-year-old can't be the same as for a teen or adult, but there does need to be a standard!"

"My standards of cleanliness had to be adjusted to the age of the child. However, if the child doesn't do as good a job as I know she is capable of doing, I make her do it over."

"I had to relax my standards and remember that it is much more important for them to help than to do the job up to my standards."

"For helpers of any age, whether kids, spouses, or adult sons and daughters, don't demand perfection, or they will get discouraged and quit. I learned that the hard way. Now I've learned to lavishly praise the parts I appreciate most and be quiet about the rest and both hubby and grown-up adult kids (when they are here for a visit) are generous with their help."

"We clean because we want order in our lives, a healthy environment to live in, and a comfortable place for friends to visit, not so every last speck of dust is banished or every sofa pillow is at just the right tilt."

If It Isn't Up to Snuff

When training helpers, the old "how clean is clean?" will rear its dusty head time and again. We show up to review a room a family member has been assigned or is responsible for cleaning. They say it's clean, but you behold an area that has only had a last-minute surface swoop or swipe. You can react (as we all have) with, "You call this clean?! The EPA would condemn this room! Now do it right. I'll be back in an hour and it better be spotless or else." In cases like this they probably knew it wasn't clean enough. All of us, whether in school, at work, or even on a playing field, often test to see what we might be able to get away with, what level might be acceptable.

If you have standards set, all you have to do is hand the responsibility back to them. "Do *you* think this is really clean?" Then give them time to answer, letting them look around while you do the same. Don't criticize or say a word, but if there is a glimmer of a good job there anywhere, mention it.

Now is the time to use expectation: "I know you can do better than this, I've seen you." And then involvement: "Want me to help you a minute?" And when it is better, not necessarily perfect, give some recognition. Quality is gained exactly like muscle, by practice, doing something over until you get it right. A job *not* done well is a perfect opportunity to show that you are watching and that someone cares enough to look over what they are doing.

Whatever you do, don't criticize! You'll put out all the sparks of the desire to clean if you ever belittle the level of cleanliness one of your newcomers achieves. This is also the single surest way to discourage grownups from helping—by saying their work isn't satisfactory, especially in public. No matter how you word it, what it's really telling them is: they don't measure up.

When something isn't done right, better than talking about it is to simply lead them through the redo. I've also found that letting youngsters "inspect" and comment on each other's cleaning jobs or rooms causes them to be a lot more careful about what they do in their own. (They learn a few things about what and how to clean in the process, too.)

"Chores should be age-appropriate, and parents should look to first see 'why' if a child seems unable to complete their tasks."

"My son asked for a fork to eat his pancake, and when I handed it to him he noticed it wasn't quite clean. He had done the dishes last night. A great chance to gracefully make the point that dishes and silverware need to be sponged or wiped, not just dipped and rinsed."

"I make sure that when I recommend a different way to do something that I give it as a nice suggestion and not a command. Children have to be treated as human beings first and foremost!"

"The less nagging you do, the better. Find things they do well and make the most of it, and thank them to the hilt! I love my girls, and we have a great relationship. We need to remember what is really important. Houses can get cleaned at some point, and they are not worth destroying your relationships for."

"You need to praise and thank children for the cleaning they did do. You can always find something good in the job they did. Always follow a negative remark with a positive one. If negative is all one ever hears, that person will become negative. Example: 'The bathroom looks great! But don't forget to catch any hair in the sink.'"

"Be gentle. We want to be firm with our children, but firmness without gentleness becomes harshness. Our kids love to please us. It is a joy to them when Mum or Dad is delighted by a job they have done well. A critical spirit will destroy that inborn sense of wanting to please. Mum does a better job of the ironing than daughter (nine years old). So what? Dad packs the dishwasher with all the dishes in rows oh so neat, plates all arranged in descending sizes. Son (five years old) has them all over the place. Does it matter? Son (three years old) sometimes puts a knife away where the forks go, but he is learning. We offer advice. We give instruction. We do things with them over and over until they become a habit. When we correct our children, we do it delicately, kindly, lovingly. Failure because of lack of effort is unacceptable, but failure with effort is a natural part of the learning process."

"If the kids don't do a good job, work with them patiently until it's right. It doesn't have to be perfect. It's more important to build up their confidence in what they can do. My husband's parents are very fussy people, and they didn't like the way he did chores when he was a child. Nothing he cleaned was perfect, and so they didn't let him do anything. As a result, he still can't make a bed properly, and the first time I let him do the dishes, he only washed the fronts of the dishes, leaving the backs greasy and nasty. Don't worry, he gets it right now. But I think if his parents had worked with him, instead of just relieving him of these chores, he would

have learned how to do things like this earlier. I promised myself
when I saw this in my husband that I would teach our kids EARLY
ON how to clean and organize their space."

Don't Redo!

"When my children perform a task, such as vacuuming,
dusting, making a bed, etc., I never redo the job
because it wasn't good enough. I might give them
pointers while they're doing the job to help them
do it better, but I never redo it. ABOVE ALL: Don't
criticize even the slightest efforts unless it's a
teenager who kicks stuff under the bed because he's
anxious to leave for the movies. Younger ones need
all the encouragement and approval that they are
contributing so don't redo their jobs. Always reward
with hugs, thank yous, and special treats when you
can. You don't want to find your child saying someday,
'Nothing was ever good enough for Mom or Dad.'"

"Do not 'improve' their job. Going behind them and touching
up their work sends a signal that they weren't good enough.
When small children are just learning, you'll have to tolerate
a little missed dust or a smudge on the shower door. It's an
investment that pays off in the long run. Everyone needs to feel a
sense of accomplishment. We all want to contribute. Frequently,
children are denied that when they are small, because parents
are unwilling to have a less-than-perfect result. Then, when the
parents want the kids to help, they're no longer interested."

"Though they don't always do the job the way I'd like to see it
done, I never go back and touch up what they do. I want them
always to have the feeling they're truly contributing, and I believe

if I revisit their jobs they'll end up wondering why they bothered to help in the first place."

Persist!

You'll have to keep at it to make it work, so don't get discouraged in the teaching process. Sticking to your guns, which many parents fail to do with their cleaning trainees, causes a little irritation, guilt, and blame at first. But it's worth the effort, so persist!

Forget about the statement we've all made so many times: "It's easier just to do it myself!" Keep convinced that it's worth any amount of time and effort to keep teaching kids to clean.

Don't Cave in at the Cave!

When the kids' room looks like a yeti's cave (as even our adult areas can look when we get busy), the time has come to put your foot down.

Here is a real crossroads of our behavior patterns in life. When there is a rule, policy, standard, or schedule, we can either face it and follow it or con and cry our way out of it. I've hired thousands of full-grown, educated, and capable adults who still handle needs or unpleasant situations this latter way—by trying to get around them. I'll bet it all started in a childhood situation where the parent caved in, or failed to stand firm in a rule or assignment. I've seen kids pout and sit in their room all day in defiance of the order to clean it. This is an important moment of education. Let them sit there for two or three days if necessary until they *do* clean it, and it will be the last time they try this tactic.

But most of us haven't the heart—those cries of woe wound us, and we rush in to help. We end up doing it all (or most of it) and letting them run free. The lesson taught here? Stall and beg and whine and you'll be rescued! Don't do it, don't cave in. It will only take a few times of standing firm before they get the message, and the work will then get done.

Don't cave in. As one child behaviorist said, "They know if they whine and kick long enough you'll fold." Many mothers over the years have concluded it is easier to just quit the fight and do it all themselves. Don't! Even accepting "I'll try" from family members is caving in. The banker, the police officer, or the contractors later in their lives will not cave in, so they might as well learn now. Make it clear that there will be no quitting or feeble attempts around your house.

Giving up on this point is simply out of the question because there are always more choices for solving the problem. If you are convinced instilling clean habits in a child is worth it, and I assure you it is, you'll seek, find, and use them.

> "My twenty-year-old called me the other day and said, 'Mom, you wouldn't believe how clean my apartment is! Remember how I didn't always like to clean, but all your teaching paid off. Even my friends are amazed I keep it this clean. Thanks, Mom, for never giving up on me.'"

"It takes time and patience to train and sometimes retrain a child to do chores, but it's very nice to sit down after dinner and hear the dishes being done instead of doing them yourself."

"Consistency is the key. The reality is that most of us are born with a preference for play. Work requires self-discipline. Which child wouldn't rather build a sand castle than clean a toilet? (How many grownups still wouldn't rather build a sand castle than clean a toilet?) Add to this that children are born gamblers. If they can get away with something one time in twenty, it is worth a try. 'I'll just give it a quick lick with a duster then go back to playing.' 'Instead of folding these clothes and putting them away, into the wash they go.' 'Oh, I forgot.' (Yeah right, like when did you last forget Dad's promise to let you choose a video to watch? We all remember what we want to!) Our job as parents is to consistently reward good behavior and make sure there are negative consequences for all bad behavior."

"Be consistent. My kids have a bucket of bath toys. They are supposed to put the toys back in the bucket before hopping out of the bath. We went through several months of nagging, stalling, and power struggles over this rule, but we enforced it and we enforced it consistently. One day, the power struggles just ended. The children accepted this as part of the routine. Now, if the kids are clean and I say, 'Hop out!' they tell me, 'Okay, but I have to put the toys away first!' It's music to my ears."

The Big Moment: You Will Reach It

As we often did on the ranch I grew up on, one winter morning my father and I loaded some cows into the truck to take to market. Going to the stockyard with Dad was always a treat. But this time he tossed me the keys and said, "You take them to the sale—I'll be staying home" and walked away. My first solo trip!

The full weight of responsibility descended after I was alone with our assets. The roads were full of black ice, and every time the cattle shifted position the truck would slide around on the road and I nearly lost control. I finally arrived and began the whole process of lining up, signing up, weighing, and bidding, and then picking up the money. I remember the mounting thrill as I got closer and closer to success, the relief of "done," and the confidence that came with it. The trust of this one little trip opened a lot of other life doors.

When the training is done, motivation complete, skills learned, inspecting over, there will come someday the big moment when you can finally count fully on your child cleaners. It will come, and it's a great one!

"I find that when children are given ownership and 'let go,' they have more pride in their accomplishment ('I did dinner ALL on my own, Daddy! No help!') and usually more willingness to do the task."

"The initial effort involved in making the kids do a task themselves (which often takes ten-plus minutes of insistence when I could do it easily myself in thirty seconds) is an investment that pays dividends for months and years down the line. Don't underestimate how hard this initial work is for the parent, however. It takes effort. It takes time. It is way, way easier (initially) to just hang up the jacket for them. This is one of the hard tasks of parenting. The rewards, however, last a lifetime."

Chapter 14
Get Some Help from Your Mate

We've been focusing on how to get the whole family to share responsibility for the cleaning, but for most women, getting your husband or significant other to truly become your "better half" around the house is a key element in getting help.

In 1986 I wrote a book called *Who Says It's a Woman's Job to Clean?* Some said it was an idea ahead of its time—imagine, a book telling men that yes, they not only *could* clean, they *needed* to clean. After offering a myriad of logical reasons why cleaning would improve men's home relationships, provide a good carry-over in their careers, give them exercise, and offer a good example to their kids, I proceeded to boost their cleaning confidence with practical solutions for how to clean better, faster, and more efficiently.

Get Them Thinking

I'm convinced that the only reason many men are still dumping the housework on women is that they've never really thought about the unfairness of it all.

For example, in the early years of my marriage, my reputation as a great cleanup expert testified that while I knew a lot about house*cleaning*, like most men, I knew nothing about house*work*. I ached to jump in and show those "disorganized gals" how an expert could square things away.

My chance came after I had taken a hard job, washing walls late at night, to buy my wife a surprise plane ticket to Alaska to visit her mother. I told her to stay as long as she wished; I would take care of the house and our six small children.

I woke up at four the first morning and confidently mapped out the great campaign of household efficiency that was about to be launched in our home. By 6:30 A.M. the kids were up. By 7:30 the beds were made, the dishes were done, and I was rolling to victory.

My wife and I were putting the finishing touches on our new home in those days, and my project for the morning was the construction of a vanity cabinet for the master bathroom—an easy half-day's work. I had just started to glue the first board when *Waaa!* One of the kids had biffed another. I ran out, made peace, passed the storybooks, and read a great story. Then I picked up the board again. *Waaa!* Someone hurt a finger. Three Band-Aids and ten minutes of comforting later, I picked up the hammer. I had started one nail when *Waaa!*—now it was a diaper to change (a cry that was repeated an intervals all day.)

I returned to work and the milkman arrived, then the mailman. I ran down to sign for a package and the phone rang—the school telephoning about one of the kids' preschool registrations. You wouldn't believe how my morning went. My building project looked like a chimpanzee special—dried glue and badly cut boards all over, and no real progress had been made.

Noon came, and with it came another surprise. Those little dudes don't appreciate what you do for them! Nap time, and would you believe kids don't all go to sleep at the same time? I've bedded down 600 head of cattle more easily and quickly than those six kids.

Fortunately, the day ended just before I did. I had two boards on the cabinet by the time the last baby was ready to sleep. The most famous housecleaner and best organizer in the West had accomplished nothing.

I had never worked so hard in my life, and I was right back where I started when I got up. I'd never had that feeling before. But women are expected to live with it every day. The week before I had three important business conferences, bought four vans with one sweep of the hand, and expanded my business into Arizona with a single phone call. But on that day I was just tired and discouraged.

I'll skip over the gory details of the next few days, but in general my half-day cabinet job, only half completed, bit the dust. A week later my wife called to check on things. I pinched the kids to get them howling in the background so I wouldn't have to beg her to come back and save me. She returned at once, and I suddenly got efficient again.

I'm telling you this story because the man in your life, like this macho man, may have never truly experienced total round-the-clock household responsibility. Short of a trip to Alaska, there are ways you can get him thinking and even eager to step up to the household plate.

Don't Let Tradition Intimidate You!

Why are men often blissfully ignorant about what it takes to run a house?

Not one reason in the world other than it was handed down. Mother did what her mother did, what her

grandmother did, and what her great-grandmother did. Twenty, forty, sixty years ago, it was traditional for women to do the cleaning while men made the living for the household.

Now most women are contributing financially to the family's support, yet few men are doing housework. Men expect women to clean because that's what their fathers expected of their mothers. And women feel guilty about not cleaning because their mothers did.

It's easy to understand why we men automatically assume we'll be cleaned up after. Mother and sister did it for us when we were babies (and beyond); janitors and teachers did it for us at school. The team manager cleaned our locker room; the city and county clean up the roads and parks after us and haul off our garbage.

But we also don't have to be intimidated by tradition. All tradition means is "the way they did things for a while." The way they did things *then* may not meet the needs of *now*. Today, men and women do much of the same kinds of work outside the home. It only makes sense that we share the same kinds of work inside the home too.

Sharing the Load: Ten Benefits for Him

Sharing the load is not only the right thing to do—it will make his life appreciably better, too, in at least the following ways:

1. **He'll have peace and a clear conscience.** Facing up to a few minutes of housework each day is much easier than haggling and scheming. For him, that means no more dodging, excuse-making, or debating. For you as a couple, it means no more nagging, bargaining, griping, complaining, questioning, and most importantly—no more fights over housework.

2. **He'll reap long-term benefits from just a few minutes each day.** Doing his chores plus a little extra will probably

take less than an hour a day, plus maybe an hour or two on the weekends. How will he find time? He probably spends that much time now on things like rereading the sports page, evaluating the neighbor's progress on his new patio, or watching reruns of *Walker, Texas Ranger*. Which will have the most dramatic effect on his family, his home, and his most important relationships? It's an easy answer: jump on the housework, pitch in . . . and then relax.

3. **Cleaning is good exercise.** Does he waste his time riding stationary bicycles or wrestling with expensive muscle-building contraptions? Cleaning is the perfect exercise—just enough lifting, bending, and reaching to keep the body in shape. Housework is exercise with a purpose, as well as a reward.

4. **Good clean therapy, too.** Does he come home irritated, agitated, pent up, and tense? A snort of housework gives the mind a chance to unwind as we work out our frustrations. There's something about improving a dirty condition that also improves our mental condition; the act of cleaning has an oddly soothing and purifying effect on the toxins of the day.

5. **He'll get real satisfaction from it.** After a day of shuffling paper and attending meetings, soldering circuits on the line, getting the runaround from the regional manager, coping with the complaints of customers, and battling traffic for hours, there's an immediate pleasure in a freshly vacuumed floor or a newly washed window, in restoring order to the home. You can see, feel, and really *tell* what you did today. Cleaning makes for a positive accomplishment in a day that may have been filled with frustrations and half-finished projects.

6. **He'll learn real survival skills of modern life.** Forget those expensive courses in surviving desert disasters or Himalayan hardship. Unless you're rich, unemployed, or extraordinarily unlucky, you have about a

thousand-to-one chance of ever putting them to use. If you learn to clean, on the other hand, you'll learn real survival skills of modern life. Knowing how to take care of yourself in your everyday environment is a skill *no one* should be without. The man of the John Wayne generation who learns to clean won't ever have to marry just to have someone to keep house. Men of the future will have to know how to do it. The new crop of women isn't going to do it all quietly.

7. **At last, he can have it his way.** Is he the one who always insists the living room look presentable? He can't stand dishes left on the sink? Here's his chance to have things his way. He can make his home as clean and orderly as *he* wants it to be—not just the way you happen to want things.

8. **He'll save money.** Saving money is part of everyone's job in the business world today. Now he can help save money at home, too. Carpet, drapes, and furniture, for example, all last longer if cleaned and maintained regularly—some things last twice as long. Your family will also save the expense of professional cleaners.

9. **It's relationship insurance.** A woman's frustration over an unfair household load can kindle smoldering resentments that can lead to separation or even divorce. Let him take part of the housework, and you'll have more time to play together.

10. **It's a chance to set a good example.** Someone in the family, sometime, is going to have to break the tradition

that it's the mother and daughter's job to clean, cook, and wash. Examples from the Dad are a lot more effective than mere theories or rules pasted on a bulletin board. Men often don't spend much time teaching and reaching their children. Sharing the workload around the house is a handy opportunity for a man to gain his children's respect and show them how to be thoughtful human beings.

Change the Vocabulary: It's "Our" House

Have you ever received a sweeper instead of that pair of diamond earrings you wanted as a gift?

Is it "my sweeper" or "ours?" "My stove" or "ours?" Do you say, "I can't keep up with the laundry?" or "We can't keep up with the dirty clothes?" Appropriating everything in the house as "yours" may indeed mean you are willingly taking on everything—especially the responsibility.

One morning on the Regis and Kathie Lee Show, a national television show based in New York, even I did this. I made the remark, "I got this off my wife's vacuum." Kathy really nailed me on this, "Your wife's vacuum, Don? Why is it her vacuum?"

Logic finally caught up with language when we finally de-sexed the language of the business world and changed "salesman" to "salesperson," "chairman" to just plain "chair." We need to get the word "woman" out of the just-as-neutral roles of home and housework. If "yours" and "house" have become synonymous, you may need to de-sex your language too. Home and housework terminology is so feminized it almost needs a supreme court ruling to abolish it.

Referring to household chores (and all the tools associated with it) in more family-inclusive language can often lead to a subtle mind-shift for the man in your life.

When I was promoting my book *Who Says It's a Woman's Job to Clean?*, I decided to do a little adaptation. I built some very special cleaning tools, and they turned out to be a great way to open a cleaning seminar and warm up an audience to the coming subject of getting men to help around the house. First I held up a nice walnut rifle stock with a paint roller mounted on it and did a rolling demonstration. I also had a golf club handle with a furry lambs' wool duster on the end. Next was a duck decoy with a scrub brush attached to the bottom, and a dustpan with a tennis racket handle.

For men not turned on by the idea of cooking, I had a hotcake spatula with a fancy wooden Porsche gearshift knob for a handle. Next came a handsaw handle mounted neatly on an iron (audiences always loved this). Last came a vacuum with Harley-Davidson motorcycle handlebars. Though I did this as a joke, some members of the audience took it seriously, because they were willing to buy anything that might help interest men in taking part in the cleaning.

My little props were believable because they were so needed!

Men Can Clean

Men can do it. Consider the fact that 80 percent of all of the professional cleaning companies in this country are owned and operated by men. Of the cleaning chores these companies undertake, 50 percent or more are performed by men. I hired hundreds and eventually thousands of others to help me, and in the early days of my company, when we were cleaning more homes than anything, 100 percent of my cleaners were men!

When I first began my professional cleaning business, I couldn't figure out the meaning of the squint-eyed look I usually got from the husband when I showed up to do a professional housecleaning job. After fifty years and cleaning thousands of homes, now I understand the look perfectly—it was guilt. The man of the house, who often passed me on his way to the racquetball court to burn off some energy, could easily have done most of the work the woman had me do.

I've carried box upon box from basements, walking right past sets of macho muscle-building equipment. I've torn out, then hauled off old fences and furnishings from houses where the husband owned a four-wheel-drive pickup and had three days a week off. After years of waiting for her husband or sons to get around to something, the female decided that hiring me was easier than nagging them.

Many times, a call from a neighbor or a distant relative or for a strong back and a few hours of time would have sent the same man scurrying to help out. "My husband will work impossibly long hours for a friend, for a civic project, or political candidate, while the windows fall out of our house," said one woman. "He will cheerfully help out anyone else anywhere in the world." If he's capable of this—if he will cheerfully pick up apple cores or return a glass to the sink in someone else's house, he is perfectly capable of doing the same in his *own* home.

Every man has a secret mission to correct some social wrong. He yearns for the chance to make it right, whether it be helping an orphan or giving the starting place on the team to Casper Ten-Thumbs. No wrong needs correction more than the unequal division of home chores and duties!

Why don't men do these things at home? There's no logical reason or excuse; in fact, the opposite is true:

1. They know how.
2. These things need to be done.
3. It even saves money!
4. They love their home.
5. They have the time.

If you truly think your men are incapable of thorough cleaning, ask anyone who knows how a military barracks is run. Men have to know how to clean—and do it—just to survive. They cope with KP, fit everything into a footlocker, keep socks, underwear, PT clothes, and dress uniforms in their proper places, polish boots to a mirror shine, iron uniforms to a knife-edge press, and clean and reassemble their rifles awake or in their sleep. They will have everything clean, neat and up to standard to pass that dreaded daily barracks inspection.

No More Excuses

We males do some of our most creative thinking when we're trying to weasel out of household chores. A common sense, creative comeback is often in order. Try a few of these:

"I haven't washed a dish in fifteen years."
"But you've dirtied 25,000—is that fair?"
**"The guys would laugh at me and I'd
    never live it down."**
"Yes, but would you ever live it down
    if your wife left you for a man who
    does dishes?"
**"No time! I have tons of office work
    to do."**
"You didn't seem to have even ounces of office
    work the week of the NCAA playoffs."
"It's woman's job to clean."
"Anyone old enough to mess up is old enough
    to clean up."
"I run things around my house."
"You might try running the vacuum cleaner, the washer, and
    the rug shampooer as well."
"I have to be careful of my back/trick knee," etc.
"It worked yesterday when you played racquetball."
"I already put in a hard week."
"That didn't stop you from driving to Indianapolis the week
    of the Indy 500."
"It's my day off."
"Tell that to the diapers."
**"With my degree in theoretical physics, you expect me to
    do manual labor?"**
"Living is a hands-on profession—housework should be a
    cinch for a mind like yours."
"You're better at it."
"I bet you could give me some stiff competition."
"Why can't the kids help?"
"They can, but they need an example to see how it's done."
"I don't know how."
"Neither did I when I started."
"My mother always . . ."
"She might be willing to take you back."

"My young boys have to fold their clothes and put them away, and they have other daily chores. But I'm STILL DOING THINGS LIKE THIS FOR MY OWN HUSBAND! What kind of example is that!?"

Back to Basics: Cleaning 101

Ten Things Any Man Can Excel At

1. **Straightening up:** Professional cleaners call this most basic of all cleaning operations "policing the area." When passing through an area, this job is a simple matter of slowing down enough to put a few items back in order. It takes no tools or special skills—just an observant eye and a bend of the back and knees.

2. **Making beds:** If he's convinced it doesn't make sense to make a bed when "you're only going to sleep in it again," there's a respectable way out. Minimize the number of blankets and covers you use. A couple of thick ones are better than four thin ones. Or buy a comforter or quilt that can serve as a bedspread, too.

3. **Dishing it out**: I love doing dishes myself—a good feeling comes over me when I see one sitting dirty, as if it were beckoning me. If you would rather reduce the time you spend on dishes, however, invest in an automatic dishwasher. With a dishwasher, you can wash dishes just once a day instead of several times. He can load up the washer and set the timer to do dishes at an off peak time, saving money and going easier on the environment.

4. **The "Man Can" (cleaning the bathroom):** Men will quickly learn that a lot of bathroom cleaning can be done by not dirtying it in the first place. If he aims at the toilet it will take care of accidents before they happen; he can pull the shower curtain to the inside of the tub when he takes a shower so the floor and rug don't get soaked. Putting the cap back on the toothpaste will take the same amount of time now as later—except by then the cap will have rolled down the drain. Hair in the shower, tub, or sink is about the grossest thing. If he grabs a small piece of toilet paper, dampens it, and uses it to do a swift pickup, stray hairs won't stick to the side of the tub or sink and clog the drain.

5. **Dusting the high spots:** Dusting is often neglected and needed in high places where it's hard for a woman or child to reach. Most men can easily reach the top of doorframes; getting rid of dust on the high places will cut down its circulation through the house.

6. **Vacuuming use and maintenance:** In addition to vacuuming, he can maintain the machine for peak performance; change or replace belts, check the fan, replace the beater bar or brush roll when it's worn, and change or empty bags regularly.

7. **Shampooing carpet:** Shampooing the carpet is really a man-sized job

(chauvinistic, huh?). Shampooing, if done right, extends the life of your carpet.

8. **Sparkling windows:** Get rid of that amateur collection of vinegar, newspaper, and cleaning "rags." Most men love good tools. A professional-quality or stainless steel squeegee with a ten-, twelve-, or fourteen-inch blade makes quick work of dirty windows. A squeegee on an extension handle will let him take care of those windows that are out of reach. With an extension handle he can do a second-story window quickly, and his feet will never leave the ground.

9. **Against the wall:** Armed with a spray bottle of all-purpose cleaner and a cleaning cloth, he can remove the fingerprints and marks on every wall, door, frame, and switchplate in his home in fifteen minutes.

10. **Rewarded a hundred-FOLD**: It's we men who really have the reputation for snappy folding—those faultlessly folded regimental flags, intricate paper airplanes, and perfect creases in our dress whites. And who can refold a road map or coil up an extension cord as well as a man? Any man can fold towels and washcloths (an easy place to start), fitted sheets (similar to an engineering puzzle to novices), T-shirts, shorts, pajamas, or any clothes that need to be put on a shelf or in a drawer. Folding is a good way to ease into housework. It can be done while doing something else, such as watching television or swapping stories.

Feed the Flame

No matter how old we men are, a little help is always appreciated, especially for things we've never done before.

A few years ago, when my wife was away attending a week-long seminar, I decided to cook an "all fresh" dinner and made a raid on my garden and henhouse. I'd never cooked many things, but I did remember my wife usually boiled the corn, so I heated up a big kettle. (I was going to boil beets and some eggs too, so why crank up three pots at once?). So I chucked the beets, eggs, and corn all in the boiling water. Timing never occurred to me, nor did color. I ate overcooked red corn on the cob with undercooked beets and had Easter eggs ready months in advance.

I mentioned my meal marathon to my wife when she returned, and the next day my daughter, mother-in-law, and three women from church were all snickering and hee-hawing, dropping little remarks my way.

Don't do this. Please leave us some pride when we do something for the first time and get less than the desired results. Here are few more suggestions to keeping the fires of domestic ardor burning bright:

- Sit down with him and decide what the priorities are. Housework can be a chance to work together toward a common goal. What you learn about compromise and cooperation here will carry over into other areas of your relationship. Take into account how many hours each week each one works outside the home, as well as each partner's access to flextime and flex-space.
- Tell him what you'd like done. Don't just moan and groan and mutter incomprehensible phrases, or expect him to read your mood or mind.

- Give him a choice of several jobs to get him started. Don't give him the yuckiest job first. You could kill his desire to clean in its infancy.

- Don't hit below the apron belt. In other words, don't try to provoke him into doing. Don't nag. Ask graciously, and he'll perform graciously.

- No guilt trips, either. That includes eye-rolling and sighing.

- Give him a break. Remember he's only a rookie. You may need to explain how to do it.

- To each his own. You have your way of doing things, so let him have his way, as long as he gets the job done.

- Don't expect a miracle. Just because he's been hoarding all that housework talent for ten, twenty, or forty years doesn't mean he can redeem himself in a single cleaning surge.

- Criticize privately. If he ruins, breaks, or streaks something, don't point it out in front of the kids, your friends, or your mother.

- Make use of the power of positive feedback. Remember how miffed you were when he failed to notice the job that took you all day? Don't make him go through that! Please do notice what he's doing, and praise him. He's going to need it!

The new-century cleaning constitution: All people clean equally!

If you need more guidance in this area, write to me for a copy of *Who Says It's a Woman's Job to Clean?* Send a check for $6 plus $3 shipping to: Who Says, P.O. Box 700, Pocatello ID 83204; or call 888-748-3535. In the next printing I'm going to change the title to *How to Make Women Love You . . . Do the Cleaning!*

Chapter 15
Other Sources of Help

So much of our search for help with home care and cleaning is centered within the walls of our home that sometimes there is a real wall there, one that shuts out the sources outside. It would be great if the residents of a home could always meet every need of their own household—the cost, savings, and opportunities for personal development would be awesome. But that is not always the case. There are other realities out there, such as the fact that some houses are huge while the number of people in the household is small. There also may be an age factor or perhaps a fear of heights, allergies connected with cleaning, demands of jobs outside the home, and other reasons for which the residents just don't have the time, energy, or ability to deal with all the rigors of home care. Single parents, for instance, are often caught up in the need to support the family and deal with all of the other urgencies of home and family care.

The bottom line here is that sometimes we really do need some supplementary assistance; we need to go to outside sources, an entirely honorable and intelligent thing to do. Handled correctly, it can make sense economically, too. In fact, I've made a living for the past fifty years cleaning for others.

When your in-house options just can't handle it all, there are at least six good sources of outside help:

1. Relatives, friends, and neighbors
2. Babysitters
3. Guests
4. Clubs, church groups and the like
5. Professional cleaners (maid services, cleaning contractors, and personal housekeepers—see Chapter 7 of *Is There Life After Housework?*)

Relatives

I put these folks first because they are the closest to your immediate family and generally know you and your home and needs the best. They are often also the most compassionate. You may have to shed some pettiness and pride to make the most of relatives who might help. Remember, nothing is more right than helping a family member in need—helping hands are holier than praying limbs, as they say.

For several years I was in charge of a large church congregation in a resort area, and this included being in charge of the welfare for the needy. I soon learned that family was the first and the best contact to make when someone was down and out or in need of any type of support. If the family was unable to lend a hand, then we went to other resources.

During this same time period, my wife and I also had foster children from four different Native American tribes, and we discovered the impressive way Native American families look after one other. If a problem arises, aunts and uncles, grandparents, or brothers and sisters step in and help their relatives to get back in operation. Relatives can give rides, a hand with special events, or during temporary disability or illness, and yes, they can help with cleaning and maintenance, as long as you don't ease into entitlement and expect them to do everything indefinitely. When you're tired, ill, badly behind, or have suffered a tragedy, letting family members step in and rescue you (and doing the same for them when they are in need) is one of the most binding actions you will ever take.

One extended family has regular workdays each spring and fall at their elderly parents' home. In one day, they can do a top-to-bottom cleaning collectively that would take them many hours and trips to do as individuals. The handyfolks of the family clean and patch gutters and make other needed household repairs; the teenagers and younger children clean the yard; and the day usually ends with hamburgers on the grill or a potluck dinner.

Another family holds occasional painting parties. Everyone meets about noon, brings their paints, brushes, and rollers, and spends the afternoon painting either the outside of the house or interior rooms. The party ends with dinner, courtesy of the person whose home has been painted.

If you have extended family with children, arrange to trade some sitting time. Watch your sister-in-law's kids while she wallpapers her bedroom; arrange to have her watch your children when you have a task better accomplished without interruptions or too many small hands in the project.

Elderly relatives (and neighbors) sometimes feel like their useful days are over. They might enjoy lending a hand with a simple but time-consuming task like mending clothes or baking a batch of cookies for the PTA meeting (on the evening you have to work late). Offer to repay by doing a task they may find difficult: cleaning a ceiling fan, washing an outside window, running an errand, or tidying up their basement or attic.

Hiring Family

Hiring family members to help can also be an advantage. Even if you pay them what the same services might cost from outsiders, they will usually put more into what they do, and they'll keep an eye on your place (and maybe even some of the children) while they are doing it. If they need the work, you will be helping them, too, and they may even be willing and able to charge less for jobs.

A teenager in the family might love to have some gas money in exchange for taking the kids to the park when you need uninterrupted time to clean or work on your tax return, or he might be willing to help for a few hours with a major task like window cleaning or yard work.

One family I know has several carpenters and contractors in it. As long as their relatives agree to be put on the bottom of their work list (when they're in between jobs or waiting for supplies to come in for a current job) they will usually help install cabinets, tile a floor, or hang a door at a lower-than-normal fee.

Are there carpenters, plumbers, seamstresses, carpet installers, or other craftspeople in your family? You can't expect them to work for free just because they are family, but if you aren't in a hurry to get the job done, they can often be a huge help.

Trade Help with Someone

When you can't keep up with the cleaning, you can look outside your household for help, either in a pinch or on a regular basis. You can trade chores with a neighbor, for instance: she hates to mop floors and you hate to cook. Or you can ask a neighbor to do errand for you when he or she is going to town, and you can return the favor when you go. I've had scores of readers tell me stories of how they used "many hands" to lighten work. Here are a few to get you thinking.

> "My neighbor and I traded work in an emergency. She needed help cleaning her house for unexpected

visitors, so I spent an entire day helping her clean. A few days later, she helped me all day. We enjoyed each other's company, caught up on gossip, listened to our soap operas, and got double the work done."

"Several years ago, a friend of mine had a death in her family, and her home was the most centrally located for all the out-of-town relatives to stay. In a panic, she called me for help. She and her sister and I cleaned that entire house in five hours (actually fifteen hours of nonstop cleaning!). In return, the two of them came to my house several weeks later and cleaned in preparation for a Tupperware party I had planned. My house was never so clean, and we ended up at her sister's house cleaning a couple months later."

Good friends, like family, have a way of pitching in during times of need. And friends with similar interests can come to your aid in many ways you wouldn't expect.

For instance, a couple I know built one of the first log homes in their community. They had decided to do the building themselves. But when the semitrailer of logs was unloaded, and they saw the huge, heavy stacks of logs (all precut and numbered and lettered to be matched with the blueprints) they quickly realized they would need help lifting and joining the logs.

Several other couples in their circle of friends had expressed interest in building a similar log-kit home, so the pioneers called on them to help on the weekends. The couples (two of which did eventually build similar homes) learned how to put together the do-it-yourself home, and my friends got their home built nearly labor-cost free. After the house-warming, my friends treated each family with a day or evening on the town, depending on the helpers' interests. They took one family with young children to spend the day at an amusement park, while another couple got a seafood dinner and tickets to a concert they wanted to see.

Another couple was building a water garden in their back yard. They had friends who were interested in building a water garden too, so the friends were happy to help with the digging and edging. Their friends learned how to build a pond, and my friends got an afternoon with two extra pairs of hands to help with the heavy work.

There are many do-it-yourself projects, from stuccoing your house to putting down a new wood floor to reupholstering a sofa, that some of your friends may be considering, too. If they want to learn what's involved (and probably benefit from your mistakes), they may be more than willing to help with the task.

Barter for Help

A woodworker saw some rough-sawn lumber in the corner of his friend's grandfather's cluttered garage. He offered to buy it, but Grandpa said, "If you help me clean out this mess, you can have that old lumber." They cleaned the garage, and the woodworker proudly took home his treasure: several boards of fifty-year-old oak, walnut, and cherry wood.

An avid but elderly gardener needed to divide her iris beds that had nearly quit blooming due to neglect. She called a younger gardening friend and offered to give her as many iris starts as she wanted if she would come help her divide them. Once they started digging and dividing, the younger woman realized there were more flower starts there than she would ever need, so she called two more friends. They all spent several hours digging, dividing, replanting, and cleaning up, and everyone had enough new irises for all their beds and some left over to give to other friends.

Your Trash Is Somebody's Treasure

If you need help disposing of unwanted items, your trash may be a true treasure to someone else—and you might get a little clean-up help in the bargain. A neighbor replaced the old wooden window frames in his home with new replacements, but couldn't find a place (or the time) to dispose of the old frames. They cluttered his garage for years until his wife's friend saw them and mentioned she had a friend who used old wooden window frames in his art projects. A phone call to the artisan got the old windows out of the garage quickly, and the artist thanked the homeowner profusely for the treasure trove. The homeowner was equally pleased to have the clutter cleaned up.

Before you tackle large clutter jobs, it's worth asking if there would be someone willing to lend you a hand in exchange for the treasure that might be amid the trash.

Minimize Guest Mess (or, Cleaning We Invite)

We all seem to have more guests than ever these days—stopping by, staying overnight, and sometimes seeming to have moved right in! We like company so much we usually overlook the added cleaning burden this creates. Whether it's made by the most welcome visitors or less eagerly awaited others, guest mess is an area we need to clean up now. We love to have people come by, and most visitors leave a good feeling, but many also unthinkingly leave a mess. Crumbs and spills, dirty dishes, crumpled napkins and candy wrappers, cigarette butts, magazines, and videotapes and towels strewn about, toys scattered everywhere—the list goes on and on. When all this is left for one or two people to clean up, it can erode the afterglow of a pleasant visit.

The biggest problem is us, not them. Most guests will usually ask, "Is there anything I can do to help?" And most hosts and hostesses are as quick to say, "Oh no, you just relax, I'll take care of it."

Why do we do this? It's crazy! We refuse their help and then spend hours, even days restoring, redoing, and tidying up behind them—not a good thing for either us or our enthusiasm for future visitors. We all have more to do than we can handle now; we don't need any more to tend. If company doesn't pitch in, we will begin to plan for less company, and that isn't much fun.

When guests ask if they can help, my lips have finally quit saying "no" and my finger points to the tools and supplies. When the queen of England or the president of the United States stays at my house, even they are going to be encouraged to clean their rooms! Getting guests to help clean up their own mess isn't really an option any more.

First, you politely introduce the standard around your home: "Once they're out of diapers, anyone old enough to make a mess is old enough to clean it up." You tell adults, your kids, their peers. You'll be amazed how the idea will catch on after you apply it for a while. Your guests will actually enjoy their stay more if they help out, because *people feel good when they contribute*. Doing work together can be a real social bonding experience, even more so than shared play. So make sure you take the following steps to prepare:

Bring out some mess savers before guests arrive, such as a stack of paper cups at every faucet; an extra roll of paper towels on the kitchen counter, and maybe one in the bathroom too; and, if there are toddlers, boxes of wet-wipes upstairs and down.

If you give them some gentle hints that you expect them to help out, and make it easy for them to do so, most people will cooperate (and that even includes kids). Inform guests when they arrive where to find the sheets, towels, and trash. Travelers always are in need of laundry services, so it's nice to say at bedtime, "There's detergent and fabric softener in the laundry room if you have some things you'd like to throw in, so help yourself." You could even add, "Grab something from the hamper if you need to fill out a load." My mother-in-law even set out sheets on the day of departure for her guests to switch on the bed. She had the right idea, and people loved to come to her house and thought she was the most gracious of hostesses.

Keeping tools in plain sight helps, too. Hands go to a handy broom or vacuum. (We put a built-in central vac in our house in Hawaii, and there is a hose and wand in every room, including the guest bedrooms.) Put a scrub sponge on the edge of the tub and the sink, and a caddy of basic cleaning supplies on a shelf in the bathroom guests are using. Include things like a dust cloth or duster, spray bottle of all-purpose cleaner, and a couple of terry cleaning towels. Ordinary cleanup aside, there'll always be spills and accidents, nosebleeds, cut fingers, and maybe even a bit of something on the carpet. Most people will be grateful for the opportunity to clean up their own messes, if you have supplies handy for them.

When someone offers to help, take him or her up on it. When visitors volunteer to do the dishes, make the beds, or help straighten up before they leave, let them!

A little good example goes a long way here. If you act like you don't care, others (even ordinarily neat people) simply won't worry about leaving a mess. When you get up from the table, scrape and rinse your own plate and load it into the dishwasher, and your guests will get the cue to follow suit.

Tiny, tastefully worded signs in the right places don't hurt if you have a lot of guests. In our guesthouse, we post the daily and weekly maintenance duties for all to read, along with encouragement to assume some of them.

Come right out and ask for help if necessary once or twice and you'll get it—and you won't have to ask next time. After a meal you can just say, "Who'd like to rinse? Load? Wipe the table? While I clear the leftovers?" After all, we all cheerfully clear off our own tables at McDonald's, because it's expected. People love to help. If you ask in a good-natured way and express some real thanks when they're through, you'll always get more help than you ask for.

"Not knowing where anything goes" is always a big hindrance to the helping process. So make sure it's easy to see where to put the trash, trays, toys, and so on. Have a rack or other clearly designated area for reading materials, and put wastebaskets out in plain sight, so guests know where to put things.

Before they leave, ask people (especially people with kids) to help pick up and straighten up. It's amazing how much faster "pick up and put back" can be done by five people than by one person (you). Have your guests make a quick scouting trip through the place for forgotten toys, books, coats, gloves, and the like, too. Things like this can otherwise cause a big housekeeping burden–two or three long distance calls, frantic searches of the premises, another trip back, or a $10 trip to the post office.

Again, always thank people profusely when they do help out and leave the place nice. They'll do even better next trip.

Remember, at least three-quarters of guest mess can be eliminated by the simple word, "Okay!" Say *yes* when a guest asks if he or she can help.

"I'm not afraid of asking those Masters of Making Messy Homes–the neighbor kids–to be part of the clean-up crew. Instead of yelling, I calmly hand the guilty party the needed cleaning tools, and urge him or her to clean it up. (The tricky part with this one, however, is being in the same room when the crime is being committed.)"

Babysitters

Babysitters are another possible source of help. At least some of the time the sitter is there, the kids are usually asleep anyway. Since you hire sitters to work and are paying for the help, it's not unreasonable to give them a list of little "need dones" they can tackle if the opportunity presents itself. Let them know up front that their job is helping to take care of everything in the house, not just the children. This is a good way of heading off the mess we find after some sitters leave, even the long-term ones (including relatives) that stay with the children while you are on vacation or on a business trip.

You don't want your child watcher to ever neglect the kids for the housework, of course, but if they are willing to take on other tasks, you might consider a raise in their rate.

"Though I do not have children, I do babysit for others in my home. I make it clear that certain jobs have to be done, and if my little friends will help me, we will have more time then for me to read them a story, play a game, and other fun activities. I give them their own dust cloth with their name on it. We get things done fast by using a timer. I smile and make a game of the light cleaning. When the kids go home, they surprise Mom by helping her too. Those fuzzy dusters are kid magnets; they like them so much. In the summer, kids love water, so everyone gets their own bucket of soapy water to clean things outside like chairs, tables, and grill. Kids like to get wet and it is literally 'good clean fun.' They learn work is fun when done with others. And I always follow through with fun activities when the work is done."

Groups

Most people belong to some church or civic organization whose existence is based on public or community service. Groups like this love to come to the rescue of a brother or sister, member or pledge, or struggling loner somewhere. All you have to do is mention you have a need (generally temporary).

When I lived in the Sun Valley area, there was an elderly widow who was pretty self-sufficient, but on heavy snow days and the like she needed a little help. A group from my church would go shovel her walk or fix a pipe. She was too proud to let us do things without some sort of payment. As we shoveled heavy snow off her roof one winter, it was apparent the old asphalt shingles had had it. "You need a new roof," I said—"I cannot afford it, no," she replied. So we had to do a little negotiating. To make a long story short, my crew and I put on the roof; in exchange, she baked forty of her favorite and famous pies. We sold them, all work done and all payments made. It was a heartening experience for all of us.

Families with small children frequently have similar interests. Moms' clubs, couples' church groups, and youth organization leaders and members generally have similar circumstances. If you're comfortable with the other members' child-care philosophies, consider forming a babysitting coop. On those days you need time for large around-the-house projects, you'll have a child-care source for a few hours. Of course, you'll have to be willing to spend the same amount of time spent babysitting another family's children.

> Take a tip from the Amish. It would take many months for one man to build a new barn or for one woman to sew a quilt. A barn-raising or a quilting bee gets the project finished in one day. These community workdays are not just about work; they are always part social and help build community ties.

If your neighbors, church group, or circle of friends need help with major home or yard projects, and so do you, agree to do some collective work swapping.

Scouts, church youth groups, and 4-H clubs are always fundraising in the community to pay for their camps, trips, and projects. When faced with a "many hands" job such as yard cleanup after a storm, taking down a fence, or moving the rocks in a rock garden from one place to another, contact them and offer to make a donation in exchange for a few hours of assistance.

If faced with a cleanup you simply can't do because of illness, disability, or a family emergency, many Scout groups and church youth organizations will gladly come to your aid. Cub Scouts, for instance, are often looking for someone in their neighborhood who needs help. It teaches the young Scouts community responsibility, and the kids usually have a good time working together.

One Scout troop puts an ad in the newspaper each fall, saying they will come rake leaves for senior citizens free of charge. If you simply don't have the time to do the raking or mulching, offer to make a donation if they will come to your house and do a yard cleanup.

No time to clean the car? School groups and organizations frequently have community car washes. The kids generally do a good job—and many times they will even vacuum the interior of the car. Adults supervise them, and the price is usually less than you'd pay at a commercial car wash. If they're holding the car wash in a strip mall where you shop, you can drop your car off, walk to the drugstore or grocery, and return to find a clean car for a modest price.

You can also take advantage of group help when it comes knocking on your door. One 4-H club, for instance, travels door to door in the community each spring offering to paint rural mailboxes and posts for a modest donation. This can be a time- and money-saver for the homeowner (no paint and brushes to buy, no time spent shopping, painting, or cleaning up). Your donation saves you time and paint fumes and benefits the club as well.

"My daughter was an active Girl Scout who earned many merit badges for different accomplishments. One of those badges required doing a housework project for an older citizen. Guess who that older citizen was? The entire troop showed up at my house one weekend. At her request, I'd filled a bucket with slips of paper listing different jobs that had to be done, like 'wash off the cabinet fronts.' With sixteen girls, by the time two hours were up, I had to think up more things for them to do. By the end of the day my house was so spotless you could eat off any of the floors. We laughed, sang songs, and generally had a wonderful time. I fixed a big pot of chili and we ended the day with a bowl."

"When my daughter was thirteen she wanted to have a party with a dozen or so friends. I put it off as long as possible and then made an agreement with her. If she and her friends would clean the house thoroughly, she could have the party. Within the hour, six of her friends showed up at the door ready to go to work. I gave them a list of what needed to be done, everything they needed to do the jobs, and supervised them. They actually did a good job and had a ball doing it. They turned the stereo up as loud as it would go and danced around as they went, all the while cleaning their little fingers to the bone. They even cleaned up after the party! I got a nice clean house, and it didn't cost me any more than a few party snacks and drinks."

When people do arrive at your place to help, make it as easy for them as you can. Offer them a decent place to start—some people, expecting and waiting for help, haven't even cleared the crumbs from the table. If someone comes to do the floor or windows, at least have the floor swept and the shades or curtains pulled; in other words, show them that you are doing whatever you can to help yourself. Courtesy always goes a long way to show appreciation.

Think about what needs to be done, and who might be in a position to do it, and you'll find your own ingenious ways to get help when you're in over your head.

The Last Resort?

Finally, though it's not necessarily always the best last resort, you can simply say the heck with it.

On my own personal list of certified reasons to clean (for health, space, to prevent waste, save money, safety, or aesthetics) the number-one reason to clean and be clean is for the treatment it earns and deserves. We treat clean places and clean people better than the dirty. If we raise the standard bar too high, however, we can treat *ourselves* badly.

In a day of greater-than-ever demand from jobs and outside activities (as well as the family), the perfect, spotless house is not always possible. When a house gets you down with its constant demands taking a break is therapy, not a sin. We professional cleaners often cut "frequencies" (how often something is cleaned) in commercial buildings when the cost begins to hit the customer too hard, and you can do the same when the psychic costs are too great.

There are some things you can just plain ignore sometimes if the pinch is too great. Windows for example—glass isn't really harmed no matter how dirty it gets. Today's carpets are so tough and soil-resistant that missing some vacuuming won't hurt them much. Dust also is largely harmless unless you have allergies. Many marks and blemishes might not look good, but they aren't really hurting anything, either. I'm not advising you to leave the dishes and garbage around for a month, but I would certainly let those cobwebs or that sagging front gate go for a while if there are bigger and more important priorities looming.

A little slippage in aesthetics for a good reason is only good sense. Most of today's household surfaces and fabrics won't deteriorate from an occasional missed swipe when you have more urgent concerns to address. Generally, you're the only one who notices a little neglect anyway.

Houses are made to live in, *not* for.

> "Don't obsess. The pursuit of perfection is frustrating and a huge waste of time. Ultimately, it's more important to me that my kids have a fun, creative, and inspirational place to play than for the house to look neat all the time. Ultimately, it's more important to me to go to the park before the sun sets than to stay home and

clean the house before we go and then only have five minutes to play at the park. Life is short. Have fun."

"Remembering what's important—your child, your relationship with your husband, the quantity and quality of the time you spend together—is what really matters in the end. Tonight, when I go into my living room, I plan to keep the lights dim and the music soft. Then, instead of arguing about whose turn it is to clean the carpet, maybe my husband and I can dance on it instead."—Melissa Balmain

---

A Few Last Words

What is my own lifetime advice (twenty years after my own children have grown) about getting help with home cleaning? What is my "If I had it to do over" advice to you about this? I would tell you to follow these simple principles from this book:

1. Change "the house," "my house," "my parents' house," or "the landlord's house" to "*our* house." Once everyone buys in, they will pitch in. Once they have a real reason, then everything else fits under the big three: Expectation, Involvement, and Recognition.

2. Don't ignore the power of "clean" to improve not just your environment but your life.

3. Get rid of all excess, and get control of what is coming in—dejunk! Forty percent of your cleaning problems will dematerialize.

4. Design and arrange everything you can to prevent dirt and litter and prevent people from tearing up things.

Reduce the opportunity for mess through the very design of your home and its furnishings.

5. Provide the right tools, and keep them handy.
6. Decide on, and then describe and demonstrate clearly, what you want done.
7. Use outside help with cleaning when you need it.

The Commandments of Child Cleaning

Most parents who have taught their children to clean, and child authorities, too, all seem to agree on what we might call the commandments of child cleaning. Always keep them in mind.

I. START YOUNG.

II. Assign age-appropriate chores.

III. Have some chores that are just expected of every family member, plus extra jobs that can be done for some reward.

IV. Have youngsters work in short installments, especially when they are young.

V. Have a routine for chores if you can—it helps.

VI. Set a good example.

VII. Make what you expect of them clear.

VIII. Teach them exactly how to go about it.

IX. Make it fun.

X. Work with them as they work, or do your housework at the same time if possible.

XI. Make sure there is a place to put things.

XII. Don't criticize their efforts.

XIII. Praise them whenever you can.

XIV. Be consistent (stick with it!).

Is It Worth the Effort?

For sure, eliminate the answer a second-grader gave during a science lesson at school. Trying to get the class to identify a magnet, the teacher said, "What starts with 'm' and picks things up?" The kid shouted out, "Mother!"

In my opinion, the biggest reason to do something about the need for help is the eventual carryover into character if you don't. Mess, dirt, and disorder alone are bad enough, but the pattern of behavior that results goes way beyond an unattractive house and damage to the environment. Its eventual carryover into school, relationships, and jobs is life-influencing to say the least. Learning to be responsible for their own messes puts people in a position to eventually help others with theirs, which is the bottom line for a happy life: service to others.

> "That's what we feel parenting is all about—teaching and raising children to be responsible young adults and experiencing the pride of doing a job well done. I'll take that over having a champion PlayStation gamer on the couch in the house any day, thank you very much."

The Three Big Ones

In closing, let me say again that I believe there are only three basic principles in leading people and helping them change for the better:

- Expectation
- Involvement
- Recognition

Build your programs and approaches for changing family attitudes under the umbrella of these three principles, and you'll meet needs and get results.

Good luck with your young cleaners, and bring them to meet me some day!

Acknowledgments

Most books and their authors owe a debt of thanks to others for some of their finest inspirations, and this is only more true of this one than most.

First, I would like to thank my wife of more than fifty years now, **Barbara Aslett,** for helping me learn how to cope with the challenges of child-raising creatively. Thanks too, to our children **Laura, Grant, Elizabeth, Cindy, Rell, and Karla**, and our many grandchildren, for the same.

My parents **Duane and Opal Aslett** taught me much, too, that I have shared with you in these pages.

My editor **Carol Cartaino,** as usual, pulled the best out of me and others and blended it all smoothly together into what you read here. Her son, **Clayton Collier-Cartaino**, contributed both directly and indirectly and has my sympathy for having to live with the aftermath of a mother focused for months on "how to get kids to help more."

A number of people went out of their way to share their life's wisdom on this subject, and to help in other ways, including:

Kay Burns, Beth Racine, Rose Fisher Merkowitz, Sandra Phillips, Martha Jacob, Jim Doles, Craig LaGory, Barbara Yochum, and **Sally Davis.**

The book's path from gleam in an editor's brain to finished manuscript, proofs, and then printed pages was aided immensely by:

Tobi Flynn, Ryan Roghaar, Meredith O'Hayre, and **Paula Munier.**

As noted earlier, a good book simply would not have been possible without the real-life input of my readers, who contributed freely and fully when I asked them. Many more thoughts were offered than could be fit in this volume, but it was all appreciated and will be used someday! The people quoted directly in these pages include:

Linda Aley, Nadine Allworth, René Arney, Mark Ashwin, Lori Austen, Gina Avila, Kathie Baker, Becky Barron, Margaret Bayduza, Jennifer Bear, Sharon Bingham, Dave Blair, Debra Bowen, Troy and Crystal Bowman, Joanne Sgrignoli Boyd, Ann Bray, David and Tarnya Burge, Jane Burnett, Stephanie Butler, Stacy Butler, Lynne Calender, Jennifer Calvin, Dianne L. Campbell, Chris and Rene Campbell, Bonnie Campbell, Nicole Carmichael, Lynn Carpenter, Marjorie Carrie, Sylvia Castleman, John and Jennifer Chappell, Karen Chelsvig, Lisa Clark, Claudia Conner, Dena Conrad, Sandi Cook, Annette Cotton, Laurie Courtney, Carolyn Cox, Belinda Cribbs, Vanessa Crockford, Karen Crosby, Karen Dale, Betti Daniel, Frieda de Bondt-Kok, Diana Dequinque, Barbara Dewar, Kris Drago, Miriam Druyan, Jenny Durtschi, Beth-Ann Eckweiler, Cynthia Edson, Gabrielle Edwards, Rhonda Ellis, Dena Erickson, Marriet Etheridge, Jennifer Evalle, Bonnie Evans, Amy Farnsworth, Jane Farr, Rebecca Farrer, Jill Farris, Natalie Ferguson, Shaun Fields, Shauna Fields, Robert H. Fleming, Jr., Lynn Fote, Sharon Joy Frear, Nancy B. Fuller, Carol Gaertner, Rachel Galloway, Beth Gehres, Amy Giles, Julie Gill, Lisa Glenn, Doris M. Green, William R. Griffin, Virginia Griffith, Beth Ann Grimm, Kristine Gustavson, Verna Hall, Sally Higley, Rebecca Hoggarth, Cookie and Kyle Holaday, Diane Hunter, Petra Huppert, Maureen Jackson, Karen Jackson, Susan Jackson, Valerie Jacobsen, Nicole Osbourne James, L. Jennings, Kristen Jenson, Evelyn Johnson, Mary-Reed Journee, Bina Kalani, Amy C. Keffer, Susan Kent, Suzanne M. King, Gretchen Knutson, Michelle Lanier Michele Law, Nancy Lawing, Melissa Lawrence, Theresa B. Lawton, Michelle Leichty, Ginger Lewis, Ruth Lloyd, Ruth Long, David Lowell, Pat Luedtke, Nichole Lumsden, The MacDonalds, Amelia Mackie, Rhonda Marcum, Karen Marinshaw, Markey, Angel Mastin, Roy McBride,

Carolyn McConnaughey, Amber McEntire, Ruth McLean, Sandy Meinking, Susan Menges, James and Marji Meyer, Helen Miller, Karen Miller, Leah W. Milton, Lori K. Mirenzi, Melissa L. Mitchell, Jean Modene, Robin Moseley, Mary K. Moyer, Donna Muller, Suanne Nagata, Valerie Neal, Lynn and Galen Neal, S. Newton, Linda A. Nietz, Amy O'Brien, Lora Otero, Julie Owens, Bonna Patrick, Nancee Phillips, Mindy Phillips, Annemarie Pond, Justine Poplaski, Katherine Purcell, Tess Rebman, Sandi Reimer, Jody R. Reiner, Christine Richardson, Avice Rodda, Mary Roediger, Barb Roman, Sherrie Sanders, Sara Schlayer, Connie Schumacher, Lydia Seibert, Philip and Desiree Sheats, Pam Shepherd, Robin Shores, Elaine S. Smith, Melissa Smith, Albatina Smith, Margaret Smith-Davis, Becky Snow, Sarajane Snyder, Linda Stacey, Elizabeth Stern, Kelly Stinson, Edna Streit, Ellen Sudbury, Holly Taylor, Beth Thomas, Jessie Thompson, Linda Thorp, Karla Tschida, Turid Sanger, Tammy Uhter, Kathryn Vlach, Janine Weathers, Christine Westercamp, Janice M. Williams, Donna Willis, Kathy Wilson, Lorraine Windsor, Cathleen Winkler, Jackie Wood, Jann Wright, Sharon Wulbern, Kristy Zagami, and Kathy Zobel.

Index